Raising Money,

Having Fun (Sort of)

A "How To" Book
for Small Non-Profit Groups

Written by Charlene Horton

Published by The May Dugan Center
who did "IT" in Cleveland, Ohio

Library of Congress Catalog Card Number 91-066345
ISBN 0-9630760-0-0

INTRODUCTION

*J*ob training, neighborhood safety, emergency food supplies, housing programs, family counseling, — these are some of the services that the May Dugan Center, a Multi-Service Agency on Cleveland's West Side provides. They are the facets of a neighborhood gem.

There are few headline grabbing stories here, no heart wrenching photographs, or publicity attracting scandals. There is just the daily business of helping people save their own lives while solving the problem of acquiring the means to continue to serve the neighborhood. How does a nearly anonymous neighborhood organization with no influential supporters, no United Way funds, no church connections, or heavy financial constituency compete for support with so many highly visible agencies also clamoring for funds?

When the Cleveland Foundation provided the money for a resource development project, the May Dugan West Side Multi-Service Center transformed itself from an organization supported by "bake sale" fund raising into an agency with a goal oriented, carefully planned, successful, fund producing program. Through trial and error, determination and hard work, a major campaign with a goal of $2.85 million was undertaken and $1.2 million of that amount raised — proving that there is money available to those willing to commit themselves to the effort necessary to get it.

This manual describes our experiences as we discovered what methods were most effective in gaining the public eye and pocketbook. It is our hope that we who have learned so much about the processes, procedures, problems, and progress of successful fund raising can offer some useful ideas to other neighborhood centers in similar circumstances. Some suggestions may be helpful, or can be adapted to a particular center.

Acknowledgements

There are hundreds of people who participated in making the "People Helping People" Campaign a success. To one and all, from the first lady who gave $5, to the door knockers, Cabinet members, committee people, delivery people, mail stuffers, clerical helpers, cooks, ticket sellers, graphics people, writers, staff and all the other wonderful people who helped in so many ways, we thank and salute you.

To those donating money, thanks for believing. To those who spent time, all who sweated and worried — we couldn't have done it without you. In particular, we thank Tom and Sandy Sullivan, Virginia (V.A.) Kilbane, and the Cleveland Foundation for their leadership. George M. Keith, VP Lutheran Medical Center, our campaign advisor, kept our spirits up and our eyes focused.

Thanks, too, to John Szilagyi at the Cleveland Institute of Art for his direction to students in their work of piecing this manual together. Special thanks to Kevin Kovach for the initial work to receive the grant for this project.

And to all those who dared to be a part of this when they didn't quite know how they could make a difference — the meeting-goers, those who gave testimony, those who shared our roots and told the story, those who gave us money, those who instructed us, those who wished us well — you are all pretty special people.

To all of you, we dedicate this book.

TABLE OF CONTENTS

Introduction

Chapter   1 In The Beginning   **9**

2 We Believe In Ourselves   **17**

3 Making Believers of Others   **23**

4 Setting up the Office   **39**

5 The "People Helping People" Campaign   **47**

6 Developing Our Resources   **67**

7 The "Ask"   **73**

8 In The News   **81**

9 Managing Our Finances   **91**

10 The Fine Art of Writing   **95**

11 When Opportunity Knocks   **101**

12 Expressing Our Appreciation   **107**

13 What Experience Has Taught Us   **113**

Bibliography   **116**

14 Epilogue   **119**

Chapter 1
IN THE BEGINNING

The real beginning of the May Dugan Center's fund raising drive started with the realization of two important facts: First, in order to gain support, an organization must make itself known. The Center had to learn to "sell" itself and its programs in order to attract donors. Second, the Center had many supporters who offered time and encouragement, but few who had the money or influence to raise substantial funds. The poor have limited access to financial resources. The financially secure can and will give to worthwhile social programs — but they have to be asked! These truths may seem obvious, but until we recognized and acted on them, serious fund raising simply could not happen.

Funded by the Office of Economic Opportunity (OEO) in 1965, the May Dugan Center began its existence as the West Side Neighborhood Opportunity Center, where people of many cultures found help. In those early days, the Center provided a variety of services from job placement to care for the elderly. Guided by the premise that the problems of the poor could best be solved by those within the community, the first Board of Trustees was composed entirely of neighborhood residents. The Center's purpose, "to ensure the delivery of social services to the Near West Side of Cleveland," has never changed, but the means of obtaining funds to accomplish that purpose has changed dramatically.

In 1969, the Center was incorporated as a separate non-profit corporation 501(C)(3), independent of OEO. With help from the City of Cleveland and the Department of Housing and Urban Development (HUD), the current three-story, 32,000 sq. ft. building was constructed in 1975. Space was rented in the building to about 15 other agencies which generated almost $100,000 for the operating budget. The Center's core programs were funded by a $200,000 OEO grant.

Although the $100,000 operating budget was adequate, in 1981 a 50% funding cut for core programs put the Center's future in jeopardy. It became evident to the Board that fund raising help was needed if the Center was to survive.

In 1982, the composition of the Center's Board was modified to include one-third at-large, non-resident members. The remaining two-thirds were neighborhood residents. The Board members had a strong belief in the Center as a means to change the lives of those who lived in the neighborhood. Pride and commitment characterized their determination that the Center should continue. So, with more foresight than knowledge, the Board of Trustees formed a Development Committee.

The Development Committee's job, to raise funds, began with small-scale projects like raffles, bake sales, and mailings. Money trickled in, but the problem was we were a minor league team with no experience or contacts in big league fund raising. A mailing list, compiled from those who had donated food, lacked people who could give large amounts of money, or who could use influence to generate high-powered support. Efforts to gain the support of philanthropic companies and foundations produced only minimal funds. We simply weren't "selling" the Center. We didn't know how.

Throughout 1983 and 1984, efforts continued to raise the $20,000 to $40,000 needed each year, and some progress was made. A useful mailing list was begun, newsletters were written, and it became evident that a major benefit was needed to promote the Center's name. What we lacked in expertise, we made up in hard work. Plenty of hard work!

As a result of that hard work and a little luck, in 1985, two contributions stimulated fund raising efforts. First, the Center was visited by representatives of a large petroleum corporation. They were impressed by the Center's accomplishments, and the corporation donated $19,000 over a two-year period to make operating improvements that would reduce utility costs.

The second significant contribution was $17,000 donated by a wealthy individual who had taken an interest in the neighborhood. Struck by the Center's efforts to help families before their problems became overwhelming, she encouraged us to tell our story to others, and to "toot our own horn". People like to back a winner, and her input taught us the difference between "selling ourselves" and "marketing to the donor". Marketing emphasizes providing potential donors with a way to share in the Center's work. The emphasis shifts from what we need, to how the donor can become involved in helping people. It is more than selling a product, it offers the donor an opportunity.

At about the same time, the Center became involved with United Way's Management Assistance Program (MAP). This program provides volunteer experts to consult with non-profit agencies at a minimal charge. We had asked for help in the area of fund raising, and our MAP advisor helped us to recognize ways to better market our services.

We realized that we had an identity crisis. Because we offer many services, there was no one recognizable program with which we were associated. We were, and are, a neighborhood center operating to help families in any way possible. Our MAP advisor made us take stock of our programs and clearly identify our assets — what succinctly were the most important features of the Center. Only by knowing clearly and simply these points, could we market the prospective donor. Our three main selling points were:

1. **We work with residents to help make the neighborhood stronger and a good place to live and work.**

2. **We work directly with 10,000 families a year to help them deal with their problems so they can achieve a better life.**

3. **We are ordinary people who believe in earning our way and helping people "do" for themselves**

On the advice of our MAP advisor, we decided that the first step would be an attempt to get the support of neighborhood businesses. We did not even have local businesses organized on our mailing list! We used the telephone book and previous in-kind supporters to compile a list of poten-

tial business donors. From this we developed a series of "Business Luncheons".
Hundreds of local business people were invited to the Center for lunch
and an opportunity to see for themselves what the Center provided. (See Figure 1)

Figure 1 INVITATION TO BUSINESS LUNCHEON

MAY DUGAN WEST SIDE MULTI-SERVICE CENTER

4115 Bridge Avenue / Cleveland, Ohio / 44113

Director
Holly K. Gigante

CRISIS CENTER / DIRECT SERVICE / OUTREACH

(216) 631-5800

Dear_____:

       The West Side Multi-Service Center is a
strong force for good in the near west side And
we believe it contributes to a healthy environ-
ment for businesses and residents.

       You are cordially invited to join us
for one of a series of Orientation Luncheons to
learn how the center serves the community.
The meetings will be held at the center, 4115
Bridge Avenue, at noon on:
          Wednesday, September 10
          Wednesday, September 17
          Wednesday, September 24
          Wednesday, October 1

       We believe that you will find your time
well spent.
We will adjourn no later than 1:15 p.m.
We will be calling you to see if one of these
dates will be convenient for you. Best wishes.

Cordially yours,

(Mrs.) Holly K. Gigante, LISW
Director

HKG/bt

The first lunch program netted only one business leader! But he gave us $500 and we were encouraged to continue. Successive lunches brought business people who saw an opportunity to support the interests of their employees as well as involve themselves in concrete programs, such as housing, counseling, education, job assistance, financial services, food, and clothing. We were shocked to discover that local businesses thought we were a government office. Most had no idea what we did or whom we served. We assumed because we were in the neighborhood, everyone knew about us. We learned quite a lesson.

Once they recognized our mission, several of the people who attended the first luncheon series helped to get the word out. Our local circle of supporters grew like the rings made by a pebble tossed in a pond, as those who attended luncheons returned with their friends. We weren't raising millions of dollars, but we were substantially increasing our donations and our contacts. More importantly, we were learning the benefits of promoting our Center.

We also discovered that people referred to us by several names and this had increased the Center's identity crisis. We had been variously known as the Crisis Center (which was actually the name of our food program), the West Side Opportunity Center, and the Multi-Service Center. If we were going to increase our recognition, we had to choose a name and stick to it.

In an attempt to capture the imagination and interest of neighborhood residents and potential supporters, the Center was publicly renamed for May Dugan. A local Irish barkeeper of the 30's and 40's, May Dugan was known for helping needy families. By associating itself with this generous woman, the Center demonstrated its continuing dedication to her legacy. The May Dugan connection stimulated the interest of neighborhood residents and heightened the awareness of local businesses. In time, the name became the May Dugan Center, a Multi-Service Agency on Cleveland's West Side.

The Development Committee then decided to look at the Center's applications to charitable foundations. Careful research, excellent proposals and accurate applications had produced few tangible results. Since fierce competition exists among social service agencies for both public and private support, unlocking the door to these resources required more than well-written proposals. The Center needed to show potential donors the benefits of involvement. We needed to develop a network of influential supporters who could endorse the Center and its work at corporations and foundations. Direct contacts and people-to-people interactions are pivotal to fund raising.

Most of the work up to this point had been done by the Director and the Development Committee. Our MAP advisor suggested that it was time to commit to this fund raising wholeheartedly. He stressed repeatedly that fund raising was serious, hard work. If we were going to undertake this work, we would have to do it with "two feet". He recommended hiring a fund raiser and creating a department to work full time on development. He suggested that an appeal be made to a foundation to finance this department. We thought this was an impossible idea and resisted it, but he prevailed.

So, in the spring of 1987, the Center's Director and members of the Board approached the Cleveland Foundation with a request for money to support a Resource Development Department. They described the programs available at the Center, the real services provided to the poor, and the need for neighborhood centers to continue into the future. The proposal was quite general, with a few specific elements which could be tested, such as increasing programs of annual giving, and starting planned and capital giving. The foundation studied our proposal and suggested some changes. Perhaps because of the Center's track record or because of the recent large gifts, our determination to succeed, or because of their own previous experiences in funding neighborhood centers, the Foundation granted our request.

In October 1987, the Cleveland Foundation funded a pilot program designed to determine whether or not a small neighborhood center could, by use of a Resource Development Department, generate more money for its over-all needs than it could by just writing proposals for year-to-year programs. They also stipulated that a Resource Development Manual be written which would describe our experiences, and be shared with other neighborhood centers.

In getting this far, we learned two vital lessons about raising money: One, humility is no virtue in the competitive circles of fund raising. It is essential to "get the word out" about the variety and quality of services an agency provides. Two, major support comes from those who have money or influence to donate. It is important to ask "where is the money?"

14

Teen helpers at "Cleveland's Own" benefit.

Chapter 2
WE BELIEVE IN OURSELVES

*I*f good self-promotion and influential supporters are the first two lessons of fund raising, then developing a "think big" attitude is the third. Previous attempts to raise money had always been characterized by a "we'll take what we can get" attitude. If there was going to be a major money raising campaign, the first change was going to have to be in our mentality.

Social workers and social agencies have generally learned to be extremely careful with money. The competition for funds is great, so every penny earned is vital. Neighborhood agencies are usually surrounded by poverty, and as a result have an "impoverished" attitude. There is a compelling need to take even the shabbiest of donations, to recycle and reuse in every conceivable way. In this business, what we lack in resources, we make up in creative management.

Of course, the dedication of the social worker is his or her greatest asset. That dedication is often the reason why donations are made in the first place. Donors believe that their gifts will be put to the best possible use, and they usually are.

Our limitations are often self-imposed. Accustomed to asking for and receiving only the "bare bones" (or less), we don't think we are worth millions. We don't even consider asking for large sums. Also, we can be so busy surviving from day to day that we don't "see" possible parts of programs that could get separate funding.

Marketing the programs we sponsor can make a major difference in funding. For example, the Center remained open at night in order to offer programs for those who could not attend during the day. This involved paying a part-time worker, maintenance help, and utilities, thus increasing operating expenses. We took the time to analyze the situation and gave these activities a name, the "Evening Hours Program". We were then able to get some money to fund it. This simple change led us to reasses our way of looking at things. Abandoning our tunnel vision enabled us to generate new resources.

This change in attitude must encompass the entire organization. Everyone involved needs to recognize the seriousness of a major fund raising effort and be committed to it. This includes the Director, the Board of Trustees, the committees, and all of the staff.

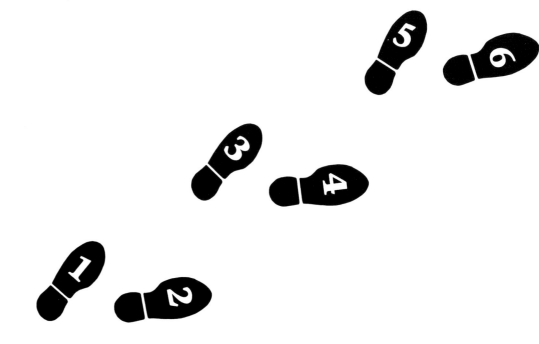

Our Director's personal list of steps to overcome the "small change" attitude.

1. Ask yourself, the Director, do you really BELIEVE in this work? Can you convey your conviction in the agency to everyone who will be involved in a campaign? There must be a sense that the people who need the agency are worth the effort needed to improve it.

2. Take an "inspector's walk" around the building. Note, in writing, specific improvements needed throughout the facility including more staff members or specific program workers, new programs, better quarters, new lights, whatever!

3. Ask the staff to make a "wish list" of anything which might help them to do a better job, from salary increases to better facilities. Pretend that money is no object. Review this list.

4. Visit at least five other agencies and observe their physical facilities, programs and staff. Measure your agency against similar organizations and evaluate its position. Add any new ideas to the list.

5. Put all the lists together and ask the staff to review them and get some feedback. Prioritize and identify the top ten.

6. Look at the top ten wants or needs and get some ballpark costs to accomplish them. This is the eye-opener!

7. Re-evaluate! Do you still have a strong belief that the agency's work is worthy of the effort needed to raise the necessary funds? This is the moment of truth. Are you, the Director, going to go for it? This is where the fund raising commitment starts! It's scary, but this is the time to decide if you are willing to pay the price of leadership.

8. Decide whether or not to take on the challenge. Are you convinced that there is money available for the asking? Are you willing to learn how to "sell" your needs to the public?

9. Present the case — improvements and costs. Begin by selling the Board of Trustees. Once they are committed to the fund raising process, the "mentality" hurdles have been cleared and the serious work may begin.

The most difficult part of this whole process was convincing Board members, committee members, and staff that raising large sums of money was not only necessary, but possible. We brought in several outside experts who made presentations to our Board. Our MAP advisor, a professional fund raiser, and the development director of a local small agency gave pep talks. They offered experience, encouragement, and advice in separate training sessions.

Abandoning what "we've always done in the past" and adopting a serious fund raising undertaking was certainly intimidating. When our Board of Trustees took a formal vote to commit themselves to our development goals of $2.825 million, they did so with a mixture of fear and courage. Remember, our Board included neighborhood residents who didn't "know any rich people". Even though they didn't like to ask anyone for money, their fear was overruled by their belief in the Center. The money was out there. Now it was time to learn how to get it!

Board of Trustees – The May Dugan Center, during our fundraising decisions.

21

Chapter 3
MAKING BELIEVERS OF OTHERS

*I*n late 1987, the Center found itself with a grant to finance a Resource Development Department, a Development Committee, a vague three-pronged giving strategy (annual giving, capital giving, and planned giving) and an obligation to write a manual detailing what we did to raise resources. We were committed to major league fund raising!

To begin, the MAP advisor recommended a special Advisory Cabinet to oversee a time specific project, or campaign. Our time period was from 1988 to 1990. The Cabinet would work with our newly-created Resource Development office and report to the Development Committee. As an advisory body, the Cabinet was composed of a diverse group and had no legal liability for the fund raising of the Center. (Legal liability is the responsibility of the Trustees.)

Created only for the duration of the fund raising campaign, the Advisory Cabinet had four important functions:

1. They initiated the fund raising program with their own leadership gifts. The amount of the gift was not as important as the fact that every member of the cabinet gave; 100% participation.
2. They established contacts with other possible donors and asked for donations.
3. They headed any campaign commmittees.
4. They advised and monitored the campaign.

Surprisingly, it was not difficult to recruit this cabinet. The Center's original supporters, the Director, and some members of both the Board of Trustees and the Development Committee called the prospective members on the phone, brought people on tours of the Center, and talked to neighborhood residents. Prospects were told there would be quarterly meetings and they could help in a number of ways. It took about two months to put together a group of people who would give the Cabinet vitality, knowledge and credibility. Some would be workers, some would be givers. Some were honorary, lending their name or public image to the campaign.

They were neighborhood residents as well as people from outside the neighborhood who had influence or financial connections, people with a strong commitment to the Center, people with political connections, the well-known and the not-so-well-known. In short the Advisory cabinet was made up of twenty-four members who could ask for, and get, money from a variety of constituents. Our delegation of Advisory Cabinet duties in relation to our organizational structure is shown in Figure 2 on page 25.

Meanwhile the search was on for the staff of the Resource Development office. Finding the best person for this job was not as easy as putting together the Advisory Cabinet.

Ideally, this person would have experience, enthusiasm, a knowledge of and a "knack" for fund raising, a personality in tune with that of the Center, and like other staff colleagues, work for very little money!

Our search took us to recent college graduates and a variety of social service fundraisers. Sometimes trial and error are the only way to find the right person. It took us some time to finally locate our good "fit".

Organizing the Advisory Cabinet and finding our Resource Developer were the result of time consuming efforts by the Development Committee, the Board of Trustees and the Director of the Center. We learned , firsthand, that patience, and endurance, are basic to any fund raising endeavor. Our MAP advisor warned us that we had to be able to "take rejection and bounce back". We did frequently!

Figure 2 DELEGATION OF DUTIES

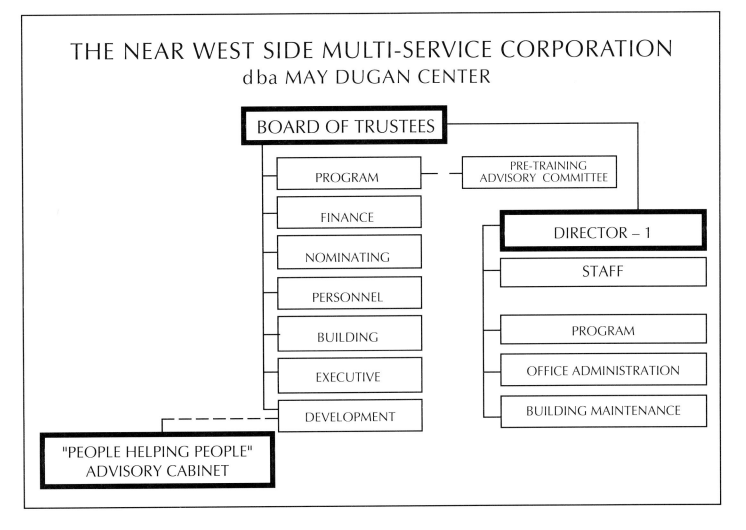

The work of structuring the campaign, defining its purpose, and naming it fell to the Development Committee and Advisory Cabinet. Our proposal to the Cleveland Foundation had outlined some general donations strategies and methods. These now had to be made specific.

Figure 3 DONATIONS, STRATEGIES AND METHODS

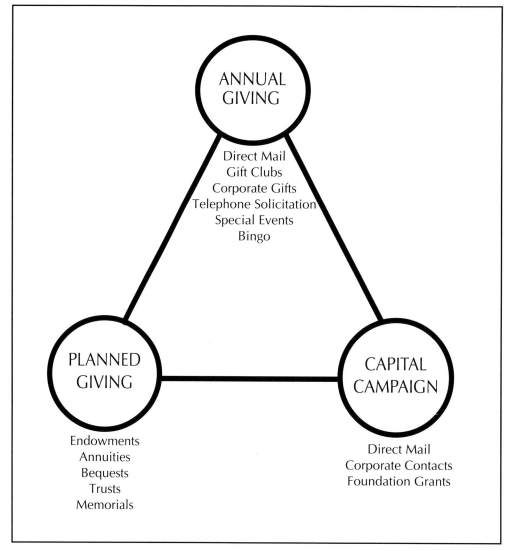

Eight avenues for fund raising were eventually developed from the original proposal:

- Endowment
- Hometown Club
- Business for a
    Better Community
- Planned Giving
- Events
- Public Appeals
- Capital Improvements
- Clubs / Business Endeavors

The avenues were the result of determining specific target groups who could be asked for money. We focused on individuals, organizations, churches, foundations, businesses and schools. We than backed into fund raising methods which could be used to get these target groups to buy into the campaign.

As an example of this process, we might first identify churches as a target group. We would then name the individual churches we knew. The third step was to figure out an approach which might "hook" the target group. A "Monthly Food Drive" in which a different type of food (canned goods, pasta, etc.) would be collected might appeal to church groups. Finally we would figure out ways to "work" the approach. A letter would be sent explaining the need and asking for help. We would follow up with a phone call or personal visit. When a church agreed, we would then send posters or flyers for the food drive. We would then arrange for the collection of the food. (See Figure 4)

Instructions to start door-to-door solicitation.

Figure 4

TARGET GROUPS	SUB-TARGET GROUPS	AVENUE
INDIVIDUALS	Core People	Appeals
		Planned Giving
		Special Events
		Endowment
	Rich People	Special Events
		Direct Gifts
		Appeals
		Capital
	Former Neighbors	Hometown Club
	Neighborhood Residents	Appeals
	Clients	Event
FOUNDATIONS	Public	Direct Giving
	Private	Capital
BUSINESSES	Big	Appeals
		Capital
		Direct Gifts
	Little	Appeals
	Neighborhood	Business for Better Community
	By Profession	Appeals
SCHOOLS	Public / Private	Public Appeals
CHURCHES	Various Denominations	Appeals
ORGANIZATIONS	Kiwanis	Appeals
	Teachers	Appeals

TARGET GROUP CHART

METHODS TO REACH

Letters, phone-a-thon, one-on-one
Extensive cultivation, visits, calls
Invitations to benefits, parties, etc.
Letter, one on one
Benefits, parties
Proposals, letters, visits to Center
Letter, phone, one-on-one, sale of cards,
Proposal letters, phoning follow-up
One-to-one, church bulletin, Sun papers
Letter, appeal, door-to-door walk
Water jug, bake sale, yard party

Proposals, calls, one-on-one

Appeal through letter
Proposal, one-on-one
Proposal, one-on-one
Letter, phone-a-thon
Business lunches

Business visits
Letter signed by colleague (i.e. Doctor to Doctor)

Appeal letter, walk, phone-a-thon
One on one, letter, phone

Speak to group, letter appeal, food drive

Letter, food drives
Letters, speak to group

This is a simple example, but by working through our mailing list and establishing our target groups, we were able to come up with our eight avenues. We tried to provide a variety of giving mechanisms. (See Figure 4)

As the avenues were studied, goals for each were set and uses for the money raised were designated. For example, money raised through the "Home-town Club " was assigned for current programming. Endowment money was set aside for the future. At the same time, methods for recognizing donors were also discussed, including plaques or nameplates for larger gifts and mugs or decals for smaller ones. Innumerable hours were spent in planning and organizing what would finally be called the "People Helping People" campaign. In all, it took us about three months of planning the avenues, targets, totals, gifts, etc. The ultimate goal of this campaign was $2.85 million! – See Figure 5, opposite page.

Hard work and planning

Figure 5 HOW DO WE RAISE THE FUNDS?

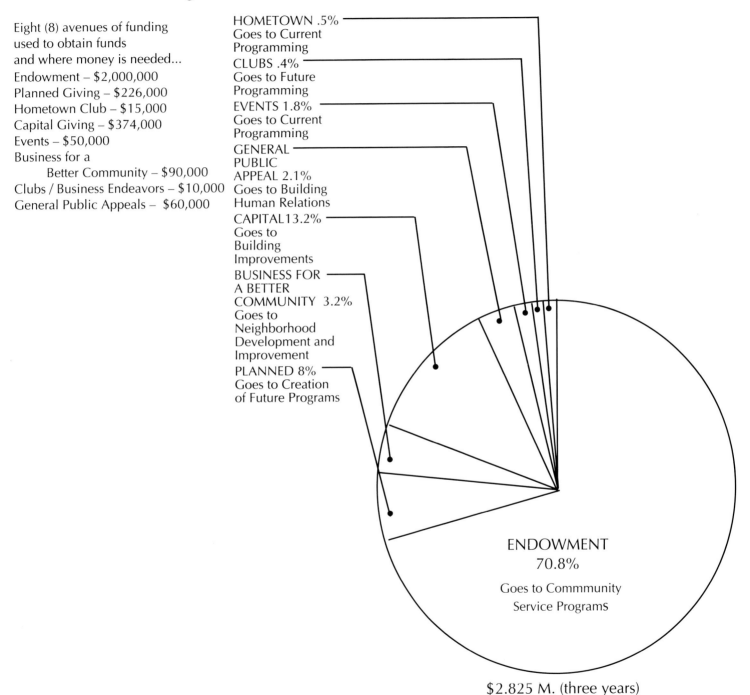

Eight (8) avenues of funding
used to obtain funds
and where money is needed...
Endowment – $2,000,000
Planned Giving – $226,000
Hometown Club – $15,000
Capital Giving – $374,000
Events – $50,000
Business for a
        Better Community – $90,000
Clubs / Business Endeavors – $10,000
General Public Appeals – $60,000

HOMETOWN .5%
Goes to Current
Programming

CLUBS .4%
Goes to Future
Programming

EVENTS 1.8%
Goes to Current
Programming

GENERAL
PUBLIC
APPEAL 2.1%
Goes to Building
Human Relations

CAPITAL 13.2%
Goes to
Building
Improvements

BUSINESS FOR
A BETTER
COMMUNITY 3.2%
Goes to
Neighborhood
Development and
Improvement

PLANNED 8%
Goes to Creation
of Future Programs

ENDOWMENT
70.8%

Goes to Commmunity
Service Programs

$2.825 M. (three years)

The Development Committee summarized its work in a homemade booklet, made a modest slide presentation and, in February, made a presentation at the carefully planned first meeting of the Advisory Cabinet .The Cabinet began studying the plan, making suggestions, and revisions.

Figure 6 AGENDA FOR FIRST ADVISORY CABINET MEETING

```
            "PEOPLE HELPING PEOPLE" CAMPAIGN
                 Advisory Cabinet Meeting
                        AGENDA


    Greetings
        - Dave Sacco, President Board of Trustees
    Introduction
        - Thomas C. Sullivan, Campaign Chair
     Slide Show of the Center's work and services
       - Staff
    Presentation of the
       People Helping People Campaign Plan
          - V. A. Kilbane, Chair Development Committee
    Dinner and Discussion
```

The work of the Advisory Cabinet included producing a professional brochure from our homemade draft, becoming familiar with the main selling points of the Center, and assembling a beginning prospective donor list. A meeting agenda (See Figure 7) illustrates some other key concerns dealt with by the core leadership of the Cabinet in the early months of the campaign.

Figure 7 CORE GROUP AGENDA

```
                "People Helping People" Campaign
                     Meeting of Campaign Leaders
                   1:00  p.m., Saturday,April 23rd
                          A G E N D A


          1)  Brochure Draft

          2)  Application to Financial Support
              Review Committee of the Greater
              Cleveland Growth Association

          3)  Filing with State
              Attorney General's Office

          4)  Three main campaign selling points

          5)  Campaign Organization Chart / & Major Gifts

          6)  Priority Prospect Lists
              - Campaign Leaders
              - 1st 10 Top Priority Prospects
              - 2nd 10 Top Priority Prospects

          7)  Next Steps
```

The core leadership also created a rather typical fundraising
pyramid plan which illustrated a reasonable strategy for obtaining such a
large amount of money. This pyramid was used to show other Cabinet
and committee members that our fund raising goals were really "do-
able". (See Figure 8 on the next page)

Figure 8 MAJOR GIFTS PLANNING PYRAMID

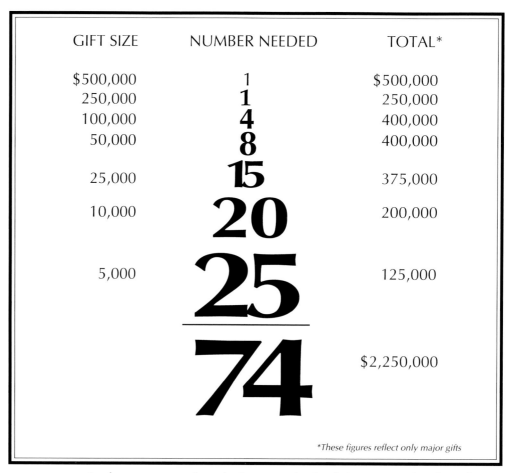

GIFT SIZE	NUMBER NEEDED	TOTAL*
$500,000	1	$500,000
250,000	1	250,000
100,000	4	400,000
50,000	8	400,000
25,000	15	375,000
10,000	20	200,000
5,000	25	125,000
	74	$2,250,000

*These figures reflect only major gifts

MAY DUGAN WESTSIDE

PEOPLE HELPING PEOPLE

MULTI-SERVICE CENTER

A National Model For Self-Help Development

At the next meeting, in June, a draft of the campaign brochure was presented. The brochure detailed the structure of the campaign, the purpose of each avenue, and the amount of money to be raised. (Once approved, the brochure was professionally typeset and produced through the generosity of a large corporation.)

The Cabinet chairperson then made a very generous pledge to the campaign, setting an example of commitment. Pledge cards were distributed to each Cabinet member, one for their own donations and another for their employer. They also received three prospect cards and were asked to sign up for particular prospects they wished to solicit. The chairperson set a three-week deadline for the return of the cards. (See Figure 9)

Figure 9   PLEDGE AND PROSPECT CARDS

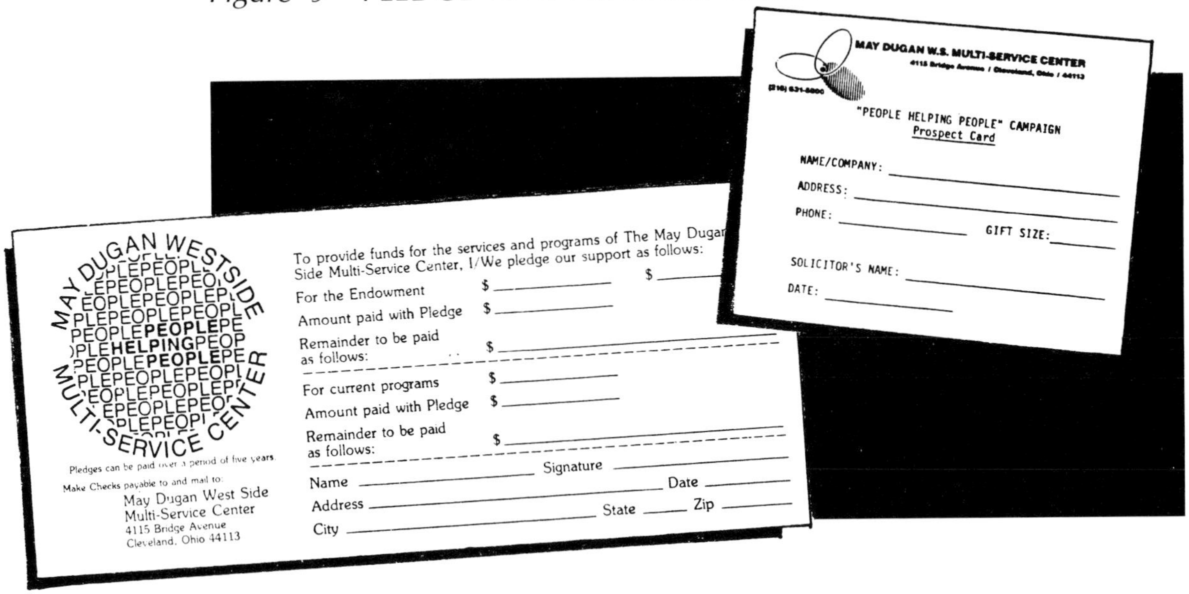

The Development Committee and Resource Development staff provided a list of past donors, large corporations, and foundations to Cabinet members. This supplemented the personal contacts of the Cabinet leadership. We were fortunate to have access to the Foundation Library, a resource center for agencies such as ours. It contains listings of major philanthropic resources and corporations, and profiles their giving habits, favorite charities, and annual donations.

We began our search by asking ourselves: who is going to give? Which businesses and foundations will support endowments? Youth programs? Housing programs? Do they give at a specific time of the year? Do they restrict their donations in any way? Public foundations must file a Form 990 which lists this information and is a matter of public record, so we researched the tax forms. Public libraries have many resources for fund raisers, including books which list grants made by various companies and foundations. Business publications often provide information on companies. Newspapers, the local Chamber of Commerce or Growth Association also have information. We often wrote for the Annual Report of a target company.

From all this information we made large lists we then narrowed to feasible prospects. For each one we made a file folder which contained the information we had gathered. We also made a Master File of index cards which listed the prospect, contact name, address, and telephone number. We then made a cross reference file of these same businesses and foundations and arranged them according to the areas which they supported. There was also a file arranged according to the months of the year, so we could check it and see for example, that the ABC Company gives to youth programs every September. We would then go to our file on the ABC Company and find the kind of proposal they accept, the contact people at the company, the amount of money they give annually, and other needed information. We kept track of our calls, proposals, and the response of the company on the index card in the Master File. This way we always had access to all the information.

We now had a Resource Development office, a Board of Trustees, a Development Committee, a campaign Cabinet, and the Director working diligently to create a cohesive campaign. We were really naive about the large scope of avenues we had chosen, but we were all committed to make them successful. The May Dugan Center fund raising campaign was launched. Our Cabinet structure looked like this. (See Figure 10, page 37)

Board of Trustees Meeting

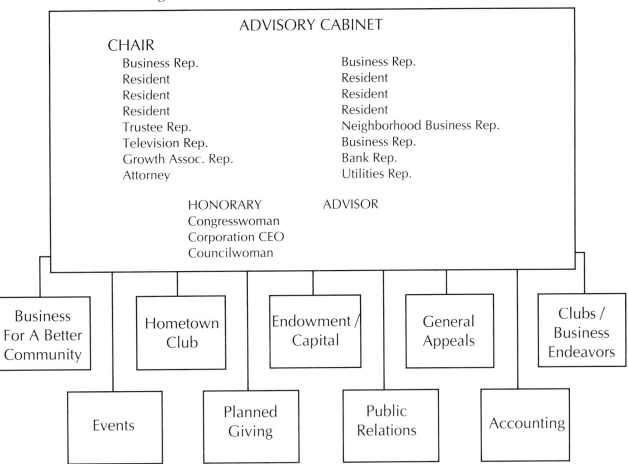

Figure 10 MAY DUGAN CABINET STRUCTURE

ADVISORY CABINET

CHAIR

Business Rep.	Business Rep.
Resident	Resident
Resident	Resident
Resident	Resident
Trustee Rep.	Neighborhood Business Rep.
Television Rep.	Business Rep.
Growth Assoc. Rep.	Bank Rep.
Attorney	Utilities Rep.

HONORARY   ADVISOR
Congresswoman
Corporation CEO
Councilwoman

Business For A Better Community

Hometown Club

Endowment / Capital

General Appeals

Clubs / Business Endeavors

Events

Planned Giving

Public Relations

Accounting

Chapter 4
SETTING UP THE OFFICE

*M*other Goose's "Old Woman Who Lived In a Shoe" had nothing on the Center when it came to actually setting up the office. We literally "didn't know what to do" or where to start.

     We found that we had to go back to the books. There are as many office systems for fund raising as there are offices, and each has its own merits. Many good reference books for methods and systems provided a base for establishing ours. (See Bibliography)

     Nothing, however, prepared us for the schizophrenic nature of getting the office rolling. There were so many things happening simultaneously, that it was extremely difficult to get organized. We were still searching for the right Resource Developer, we were trying to locate space and office equipment, and we were beginning to plan for the campaign. We had plenty to do, but assigning jobs and getting priorities ordered just seemed to happen on an "as needed" basis.

As a result of our experiences, we suggest the following method.

1. After the physical necessities are met, (office space, telephones, computers, files, etc.) a PLAN OF GOALS AND ACTIONS should be drawn up. This plan is a general outline of where each campaign avenue is going and how to get there. It contains rough ideas and provides a general focus for an avenue as suggested in Figure 11.

Figure 11 EXAMPLE PLAN OF GOALS AND ACTION (An Example)

Local Business Development Plan – Year One

Problem: Lack of neighborhood business support to Center
Strategy:To develop a Business for a Better Community Support system

Activities*:	1st Quarter		2nd Quarter		3rd Quarter		4th Quarter	
Produce a BBC 'tool'	1	500cp						
Visit 75 new businesses	20	18	30	31	15		10	
Produce donor decal	1	500cp						
Host 4 business lunches for 100 people	1/25	1/9	1/25	2/25	1/25		1/25	
Impact (Goal):								
$20,000 raised							20,000	
43 new donors	10	7	20	20	3		10	
140 Total business donors (including current ones)	15	14	30	22	70+		25	

*Activities assume planning details, ie. who-to-visit-lists, calls, thank yous, etc.
+General Appeal to current supporters detailed in Appeal Planning page.

2. CROSS-REFERENCING system must be created so that information about large donors, their contributions, dates, and habits of giving can be tracked. Although we use a card-file system organized by month for application, types of giving, etc., computer programs may help to create the kind of information base needed.

3. MAILING LISTS and lists of contacts must be compiled. This is a never-ending job, as the lists must constantly be updated and revised. We could easily keep one person busy just researching possible contacts at the Foundation Library.

4. Using current mailing lists, a NEWSLETTER should be sent on a regular schedule. This keeps the Center in touch with donors and reaffirms the good use of contributions.

5. There is a tremendous amount of literature which must be created and organized. BROCHURES on each avenue have to be written, PLEDGE CARDS designed, PRESS RELEASES composed. AGENCY HISTORY, DOCUMENTS, PHOTOS, PROGRAM DESCRIPTIONS, and general information on the agency must be written and made available for the campaign. Samples of other forms of writing should be collected and filed for reference, such as thank you notes, news releases, letters and proposals. (See Chapter 10 - The Fine Art of Writing.)

6. Someone must MATCH the job to the worker! Making "TO DO" lists of activities and assigning staff and / or volunteers to complete them is an important job in managing the office. Often there are tedious, little jobs that need to be done, such as taking copy to the printer, or mailing reminders to committee members, or updating files. These jobs are important, but cannot be accomplished if those available to work don't know what needs to be done.

One way we kept everyone who worked in the Resource Development Department focused was to make a calendar which covered most of one wall of the office. The calendar charted the combined goals and activities of each avenue of the campaign according to the month of the year. A "TO DO" list was posted on the door which noted activities which needed to be done immediately concerning the big calendar. The calendar was a reminder not only of where we were, but of how far we had come.

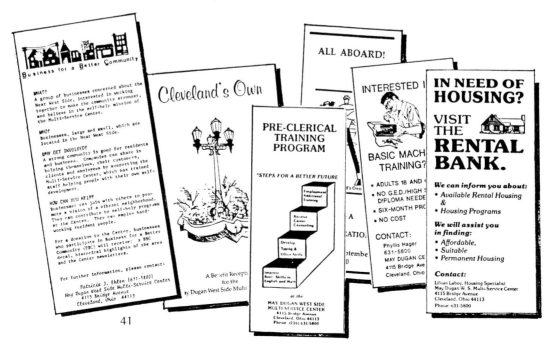

Figure 12 CALENDAR OF CAMPAIGN GOALS AND ACTIVITIES

	JAN	FEB	MARCH	APRIL	MAY	JUNE	JULY	AUG
HTC HOMETOWN CLUB	DO BROCHURE	COM. MTG.	SPEAK TO GROUP ABOUT HTC GOAL 50 MEMBERS	COM. MTG TROLLY TOUR INVITES SENT	TROLLY TOUR	DROP OFF POSTERS TO 50 CHURCHES / 75 MEMBERS		100 MEMB
BBC BUS FOR BETTER COMM.	VISIT 20 BUSINESSES	VISIT 10 BUSINESSES	BUSINESS LUNCH 20 NEW BUS DONORS	VISIT 20 BUS	BUSINESS LUNCH / 60 BUS. DONORS	VISIT 20 BUS WALK DOOR TO DOOR TO 100 NEIGH. BUS FOR NDDF	BUSINESS LUNCHES	VISIT 20 / 100 BUSIN DONORS
EVENTS		VALENTINE'S RAFFLE		BAKE SALE	MAIL NDDF INFO TO NEIGHBORS	NDDP WALK DOOR-TO-DOOR		YARD PARTY $20,000 CLEV. OWN II
DIRECT GIFTS		EACH CAB. PICKS 2 PROS. EACH		BRING 6 PEOPLE TO VISIT CENTER		$150,000 GOAL		
PLANNED GIVING	RESEARCH PROSPECTS	RESEARCH CONTINUES	MEET W/2 PEOPLE WHO DO PLANNED GIVING		PRODUCE A BROCHURE		(50 PROSPECTS) PROSPECT BOOK COMPLETE	
CAPITAL		SEND 3 PROPOSALS OUT	SEND PROPOSAL TO CLOROX		FOLLOW-UP W/CLOROX $15000			
CLUES/ BUS. ENDEAVORS	—	—	PREPARE MOTHER'S DAY CARD APPEAL MAIL APPEAL		$350 ON MOTHER'S DAY APPEAL		SELL T-SHIRTS AT YARD PARTY	
APPEALS			ASK 15 PEOPLE TO SIGN APPEAL LETTERS	PREPARE APPEAL LETTER	DISTRIBUTE APPEAL LETTER TO BE SIGNED	MAIL APPEAL LETTER		
PUBLICITY	NEWSLETTER ARTICLE IN SUN NEWS		1 RADIO SPOT	NEWSLETTER		ARTICLE IN PD	NEWSLETTER	MAG. FEATURE

The calendar also provided visible evidence of the activities of the campaign, and separated them from the goals. There were so many activities, they often took on a life of their own. It was easy to get bogged down filling out timesheets, calling volunteers, working on the files and attending meetings. But we learned to prioritize. Our ultimate goal was to raise money! Using planning sheets, the calendar, delegating jobs, and organizing activities were all means (tools) to that end.

In the early stages, the work of coordinating the office was done by the Director of the Center. Once we hired the Resource Development staff, most of the responsiblities shifted to them. (See Figure 13)

Figure 13 JOB DESCRIPTIONS

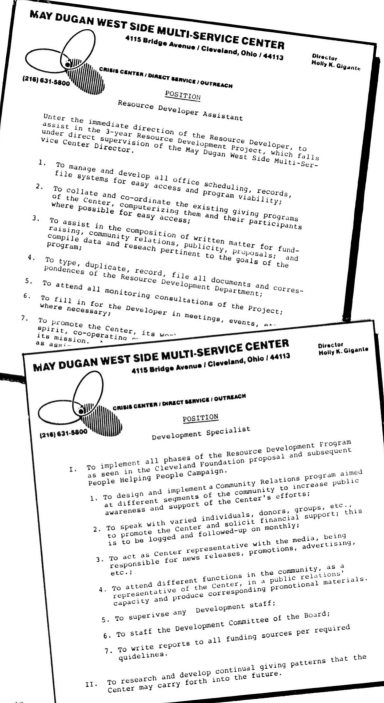

MAY DUGAN WEST SIDE MULTI-SERVICE CENTER
4115 Bridge Avenue / Cleveland, Ohio / 44113

Director
Holly K. Gigante

CRISIS CENTER / DIRECT SERVICE / OUTREACH

(216) 631-5800

POSITION

Resource Developer Assistant

Unter the immediate direction of the Resource Developer, to
assist in the 3-year Resource Development Project, which falls
under direct supervision of the May Dugan West Side Multi-Service Center Director.

1. To manage and develop all office scheduling, records,
   file systems for easy access and program viability;

2. To collate and co-ordinate the existing giving programs
   of the Center, computerizing them and their participants
   where possible for easy access;

3. To assist in the composition of written matter for fundraising, community relations, publicity, proposals; and
   compile data and reseach pertinent to the goals of the
   program;

4. To type, duplicate, record, file all documents and corres-
   pondences of the Resource Development Department;

5. To attend all monitoring consultations of the Project;

6. To fill in for the Developer in meetings, events, et-
   where necessary;

7. To promote the Center, its wo-
   spirit, co-operating
   its mission.
   as assi-

MAY DUGAN WEST SIDE MULTI-SERVICE CENTER
4115 Bridge Avenue / Cleveland, Ohio / 44113

Director
Holly K. Gigante

CRISIS CENTER / DIRECT SERVICE / OUTREACH

(216) 631-5800

POSITION

Development Specialist

I. To implement all phases of the Resource Development Program
   as seen in the Cleveland Foundation proposal and subsequent
   People Helping People Campaign.

   1. To design and implement a Community Relations program aimed
      at different segments of the community to increase public
      awareness and support of the Center's efforts;

   2. To speak with varied individuals, donors, groups, etc.,
      to promote the Center and solicit financial support; this
      is to be logged and followed-up on monthly;

   3. To act as Center representative with the media, being
      responsible for news releases, promotions, advertising,
      etc.;

   4. To attend different functions in the community, as a
      representative of the Center, in a public relations'
      capacity and produce corresponding promotional materials.

   5. To superivse any Development staff;

   6. To staff the Development Committee of the Board;

   7. To write reports to all funding sources per required
      guidelines.

II. To research and develop continual giving patterns that the
    Center may carry forth into the future.

43

Just being able to analyze the requirements of the Resource Development office clearly, and write job descriptions was an accomplishment.

Some of our daily schedules were truly grueling. Our lack of experience meant that we often took the long way to get things done, until we discovered that there were easier ways. Our journal entries illustrate not only the many jobs we did but the scope of the avenues we were trying to manage.

Figure 14 JOURNAL ENTRIES

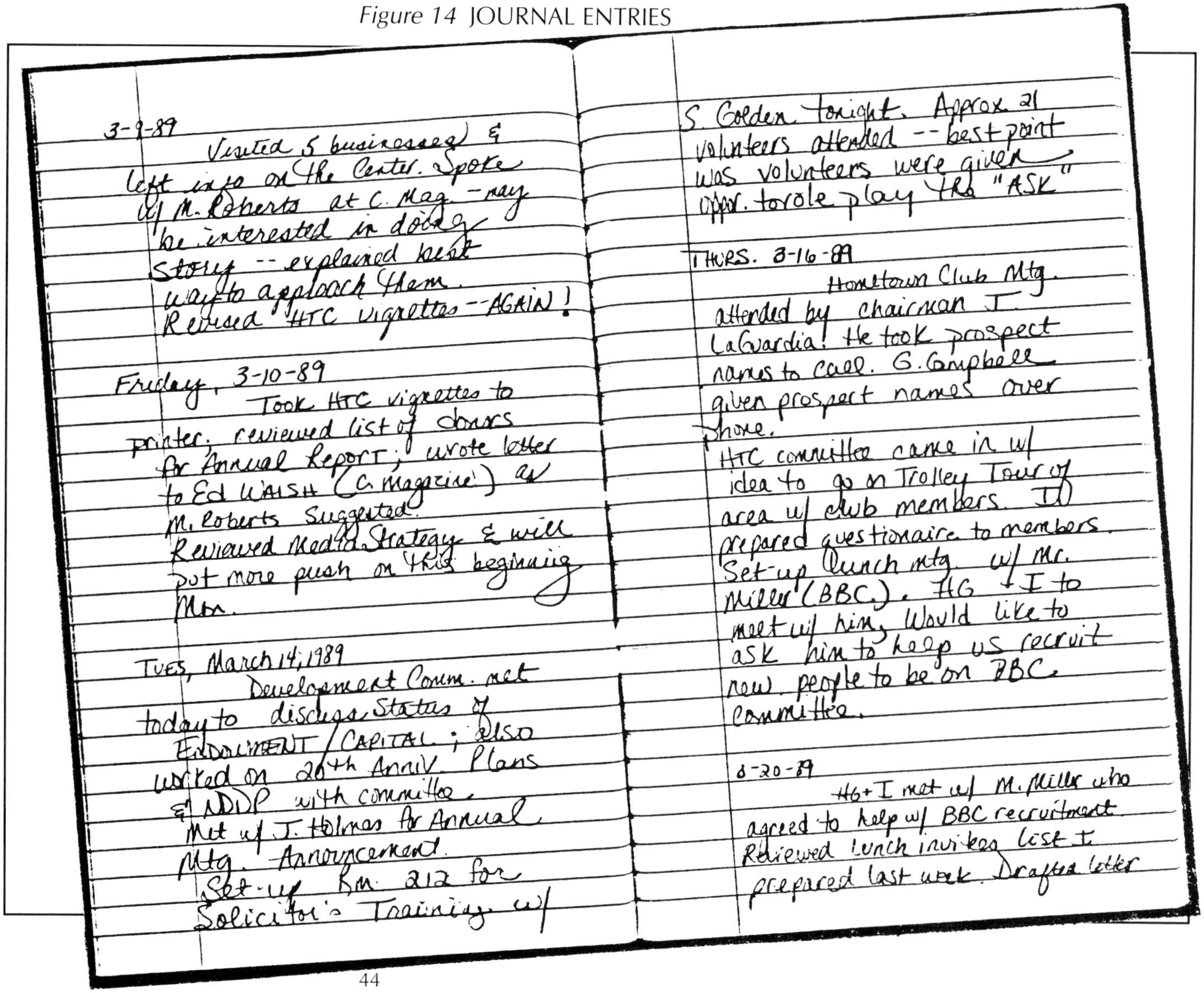

3-9-89
Visited 5 businesses &
left info on the Center. Spoke
w/ M. Roberts at C. Mag. - may
be interested in doing
story -- explained best
way to approach them.
Revised HTC vignettes -- AGAIN!

Friday, 3-10-89
Took HTC vignettes to
printer, reviewed list of donors
for Annual Report; wrote letter
to Ed WALSH (C. Magazine) as
M. Roberts suggested.
Reviewed Media Strategy & will
put more push on this beginning
Mon.

TUES, March 14, 1989
Development Comm. met
today to discuss status of
ENDOWMENT / CAPITAL; also
worked on 20th Anniv. Plans
& NDVP with committee.
Met w/ J. Holmes for Annual
Mtg. Announcement.
Set-up Rm. 212 for
Solicitor's Training w/
S. Golden tonight. Approx 21
volunteers attended -- best point
was volunteers were given
oppor. to role play the "ASK"

THURS. 3-16-89
Hometown Club Mtg.
attended by chairman J.
LaGuardia! He took prospect
names to call. G. Campbell
given prospect names over
phone.
HTC committee came in w/
idea to go on Trolley Tour of
area w/ club members. I
prepared questionaire to members.
Set-up lunch mtg. w/ Mr.
Miller (BBC). HG + I to
meet w/ him, would like to
ask him to help us recruit
new people to be on BBC
committee.

3-20-89
HG + I met w/ M. Miller who
agreed to help w/ BBC recruitment.
Reviewed lunch invitee list I
prepared last week. Drafted letter

The most important aspects of setting up the office can be boiled down to plan, plan, and plan some more, and learn to prioritize activities which accomplish the plan. Our Resource Development office has evolved from confusion to competence as the result of the right combination of people and these ideas. It was not easy, and we made some mistakes, but in the end, we pulled it together. Looking back, an eight avenue campaign was probably too ambitious. That in itself contributed to our planning difficulties. On the positive side, all the people who worked in the Resource Development office became familiar with all aspects of the campaign. So, when a job needed to be done, there was someone who could do it.

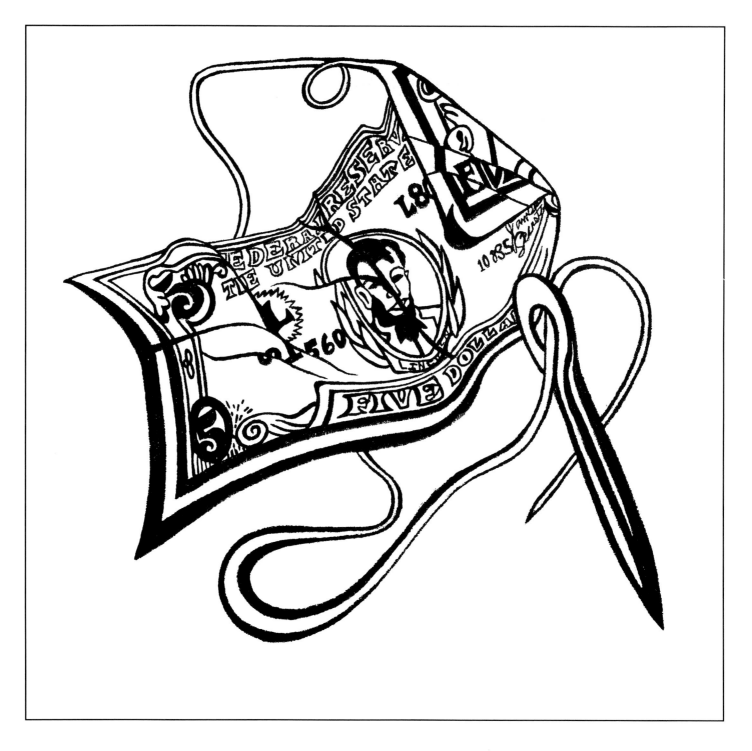

Chapter 5
THE PEOPLE HELPING PEOPLE CAMPAIGN

*O*ur proposal to the Cleveland Foundation was based on three types of fund raising: annual, capital, and planned giving, to raise funds for today, tomorrow, and the future. Creating a plan which would accomplish this objective was at once frightening, exciting and overwhelming.

47

Our avenues of giving evolved as we honed in on target groups. (See Chapter 6, Developing Our Resources.) We tried to "tailor make" ways of giving which would be attractive to different groups of potential supporters. This plan had its good and bad aspects. It was good to focus on specific groups, and to provide diverse methods of support. It was also very difficult to effectively manage eight different fund raising avenues simultaneously. The "People Helping People" campaign was comprised of the following avenues:

Endowment / Direct Gifts
Planned Giving
Events
Hometown Club -HTC
Business for a Better Community - BBC
Public Appeals
Clubs / Business Endeavors
Capital Improvements

Sub-committees were organized to supervise and develop these avenues.

While these particular avenues seemed the most advantageous for us, they might not be for every agency. Individual agencies should look carefully at their own character and potential constituency to determine which fund raising methods are suitable. For some, one avenue will become the whole campaign. Becoming knowledgeable about the variety of ways in which money may be raised is essential. Read and re-read some of the many books on fund raising. An awareness of effective fund raising methods makes it possible for an agency to choose the ones most appropriate for them. This investment in preparation pays off in the planning and implementation of a fund raising campaign.

A description of each of our avenues follows. While some avenues have been more successful than others, together they make a complete picture of what we tried to do, how we did it, and why.

DIRECT GIFTS / ENDOWMENT

Endowment donations are made to a separate fund, and only the interest is used for things such as operations, scholarships, etc. It can be a "trust" separate from the regular books or an account within the books. If we could get $2 million in an endowment at 10% interest, we would have $200,000 annually to operate the Center! Were we discouraged by the fact that very few small agencies ever undertake endowment programs? Certainly not! We hoped, in three years time, to raise 70.8% of our $2.825 million goal through our endowment building efforts.

Several Advisory Cabinet and Board members established the endowment through their own donations and close personal contacts. We had no real Endowment Solicitation Committee. We relied on Cabinet members to do what they could.

Ignorance is truly bliss! Within six months we realized that the "E" word was the bane of our existence. Some of the general public has a negative attitude about endowments and does not like to give to them. Our first brochure had focused on building our endowment and listed all the programs which could be supported by endowment funds, but many people would not give to a strict endowment fund. Some offered donations to individual programs or general operating expenses over specific time frames, but refused to support an endowment which would "make the bank rich". We were very naive to put so much of our goal in this avenue, but $200,000 annual income was a powerful incentive.

Eventually we realized that our approach was going to have to change. We rewrote our brochure, changing the emphasis to direct gifts to support specific programs. We did not abandon our endowment, we merely made it easier for donors to choose the kind of gift they wanted to make, either to the endowment or a current program. We actually eliminated the word "endowment" from our second brochure. In that way, if a donor gave money without specifying a purpose, we could ask if we could put the donation in the endowment fund. Some agreed, some did not. Or, if an individual seemed amenable, we asked directly for a donation to our endowment fund.

There were several flaws in our planning for this avenue. Our staff had little background in endowments, and we had to learn how to set one up while we searched for contributions. Our solicitors from the Cabinet had limited contacts with people who fund endowments. We had difficulty putting proposals together properly when we did find prospective donors.

We were unaware of the tremendous competition for endowment

funds, and were essentially unknown in the financial circles which did support them. We discovered that foundations tend to give to well established, high-profile endowments like universities and institutions. Some refuse to give to endowments entirely. We learned that an endowment program alone can be very successful, but it is difficult for a small center to start.

Would we do it again? Absolutely. We had originally put the bulk of the campaign goal, $2,000,000 in the Direct Gift / Endowment avenue. While we did not raise near that amount, we now have an endowment worth over $250,000 that we did not have three years ago. We will continue to build it as quickly as we can, understanding the cultivation and effort needed. However, if we had it to do over, we would research donors, get more solicitors to concentrate only on the endowment, make a reasonable goal and spend one year working only on it.

PLANNED GIVING

Planned giving means the giving of gifts through bequests, life insurance,memorials, charitable trusts, and the like. A donor gives a gift that comes due in time. This type of giving is usually associated with large organizations and colleges and is a very traditional method of giving.

We learned about planned giving by reading, going to workshops, and talking with professional fund raisers who had knowledge in this area. We obtained brochures and packets from universities and hospitals about their planned giving program. Our sources told us that this was a full-time job (like most of the avenues the Center undertook), and they were right! We invested about 5% of our time on planned giving, and our rate of success corresponded.

The Planned Giving Committee was made up of people who were involved in the Center. They included a former Board member, a current neighborhood resident and friend of the Center, and several long term donors. In this particular combination of people we had an attorney, people well-versed in the technical aspects of life insurance bequests, and financial experts. Finding the right group of people for this committee is very important for two reasons. One, since gifts are donated over time, perhaps in the form of an insurance policy, it is necessary for committee members to understand the legalities of

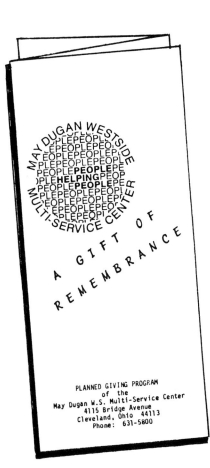

MAY DUGAN WESTSIDE
PEOPLE HELPING PEOPLE
MULTI-SERVICE CENTER

A GIFT OF REMEMBRANCE

PLANNED GIVING PROGRAM
of the
May Dugan W.S. Multi-Service Center
4115 Bridge Avenue
Cleveland, Ohio 44113
Phone: 631-5800

planned giving, especially the tax implications. And two, a committee made up of knowledgeable professionals lends credibility to the program.

The committee met monthly in the beginning. It examined numerous kinds of giving programs and was given some training in how to solicit funds in this sometimes delicate area. It also reviewed different methods to approach prospective donors, from letters and birthday cards to visits and direct asking. With the staff, they also developed a list of about 100 people who could be approached for a potential gift. A donor who will remember us in his or her will demonstrates conviction in the Center and its future. Only donors who were well acquainted with the Center and with whom a special relationship had been developed were approached for this kind of contribution. Prospect forms (Figure 15) helped guide our reference information about such candidates. We kept these in a special binder. The committee also developed an informational brochure to be used in their presentation.

Figure 15 PROSPECT FORM

MAY DUGAN M. S. CENTER
PLANNED GIVING: PROSPECT FORM

PROSPECT'S FULL NAME:

HOME ADDRESS: (City,State,Zip)

BUSINESS ADDRESS:

HOME PHONE:

BUSINESS TITLE: WORK PHONE:

GENERAL INFO:
BIRTHDATE: OCCUPATION:

MARITAL STATUS: MARRIED   NICKNAME:

SPOUSE'S NAME: DIVORCED   SINGLE   WIDOW

SPOUSE'S OCCUPATION:

RELIGIOUS AFFILIATIONS: DATE OF BIRTH:

PROFESSIONAL AFFILIATIONS: HOBBIES:

EDUCATION   (NAME)

(COURSE/DEGREE)

(YEAR)

CHILDREN: (NAME)   (SEX)   (BIRTHDATE)   (NOTES: ie., college,etc.)

ESTIMATED ANNUAL INCOME: $

RECENT GIFTS TO CENTER: (YEAR/AMOUNT/PURPOSE)   ESTIMATED NEW WORTH: $

OTHER ORG. GIFTS (YEAR/AMOUNT/PURPOSE)

KEY LINK TO ORGANIZATION:

The brochure explained the planned giving program we had chosen for the Center. In it a "Gift of Remembrance" was described as a bequest, a life insurance policy or portion of the policy, a charitable trust, or a memorial. Information on each of these gifts was included as well as a statement which assured the reader that an annual audit of our books would be made available to the public, and that all records were kept independently and in strict confidence at the Center.

The Planned Giving program was mentioned regularly in our newsletter so that our general constituency could be made aware of it.

Soliciting planned giving donations is a delicate matter and the results are not immediately apparent. For example, a woman who has been part of the community for years, and who was asked to help with another avenue of the campaign is a planned giving prospect. She was approached by a committee member and a staff member and asked for her opinion on our planned giving brochure. During the visit, they discussed the importance of preserving the Center for the future, and the committee member mentioned her own decision to donate a portion of her insurance to the Center and her hope that others would do the same, since most people have insurance. In this way, a potential donor was made aware of this method of contributing to the Center. The important thing about planned giving is that a source should never be underestimated. A $5-per-year donor could leave a $5,000 or more life insurance policy, so be attentive to each donor.

We have not received any bequests yet, but have begun a good foundation. We did receive gifts of $10 - $200 in the form of "Memorials", made in honor of anniversaries, birthdays, holidays, or to commemorate the death of a loved one. We sent a card (see Figure 16) to the honored person or family telling them that a gift had been received and from whom, and a thank you to the donor. We also announced the remembrances in our newsletter. During the campaign, about $730 was given in this way. Our original goal for this avenue was $226,000.

Figure 16 MEMORIALS & REMEMBRANCES

EVENTS

Cleveland's "movers and shakers" are frequently featured on the newspaper's society pages at benefits designed to raise money for charitable causes. We never dreamed that a small agency like the Center could ever make it to the big league events of fund raising, but we did! Of course, it took years of trying, scores of dedicated volunteers, and enormous investments of time, energy, and tension!

This avenue was divided into local community events and general events. Our community events were, and continue to be, very important because the Center is run by and for neighborhood people. The general public events were designed to involve new people from a diverse, city-wide area, in the Center. Since Events is the one avenue through which we surpassed our goal of $50,000 and raised over $69,000 it should be looked at in detail.

☞ 1. COMMUNITY EVENTS

We had numerous community fund raisers. Bake sales, car washes, yard parties, and garage sales were good ways to raise money and involve local people in the Center. Community events often acted as levers for other donations. When people outside the neighborhood saw the local community working together toward self- sufficiency, they often responded with donations of their own.

Community events did not generate large sums of money. Our most recent "Giant Yard Sale" produced about $1,500 in profits, the largest amount we have raised in this way. Volunteers and staff members usually directed these community events, and they were carefully evaluated, just as the larger events were, so that they could be improved in the future.

☞ 2. GENERAL PUBLIC EVENTS

Our general public events began with a series of teas designed to bring affluent suburban women into the Center. The first Tea was the result of networking on the part of our core supporters. Women on the Board of Trustees and various committees contacted their friends and invited them to "Come to the Center, and bring a friend!" The Teas were really the best method to find volunteers who eventually formed the core of our big Events Committee.

Figure 17 EVALUATION OF TEA

Tea - Wednesday, August 24
A tea was scheduled and held on Wednesday, August 24, to try to cultivate a group of people who could get excited about helping put on our first large Cleveland's Own benefit. Our goal was to get volunteers for the Center's regular programs, as well as get about 10 women signed up to assist with the benefit. The room for the tea was set up on Tuesday afternoon. V.A. borrowed card tables, table cloths and dishes for the tea. This was a nice touch but not really neccessary. It was a lot of work for a small "event." We had name tags on a table in the lobby with the peoples' names already on them. Approximately 20-25 women attended the tea. (We need to keep a better count of this next time, by having them all fill out volunteer interest forms.) Twelve women filled out the volunteer interest forms to help out the Center. It is vital we get them working as soon as possible and get them involved.

Becky and I took them on tours of the building while Sandy and V.A. made sure the food and beverages were ready. This worked out really well. V.A., Holly, Sandy, Kathy, and Mary C. (volunteer from the neighborhood) spoke. The women seemed interested and this worked out really well. The next tea should be done simpler without so much work. It will be as successful and a better use of time.

Submitted by P.J.E.

A very nervous, inexperienced Events Committee then began to plan our first major public event. Subcommittees were formed to answer the key questions: What kind of benefit will be unusual, appealing, and fun? How many people will we be able to accommodate? What date has not already been snapped up by Cleveland's other charitable organizations? What is the goal? How will we realize it? Who, if anyone, can

underwrite some of the costs? Will businesses or caterers donate their services? As Joan Flanagan says in her book, Grassroots Fundraising, we learned to "do the arithmetic first!"
(See Figure 18)

Figure 18 CLEVELAND'S OWN BENEFIT — BUDGET WORKSHEET

CLEVELAND'S OWN BENEFIT
"DO ARITHMETIC FIRST!"

PROFIT GOAL $_____

COSTS:

HALL ____ TENT: _____
SECURITY: ____ BATHROOMS: ____
INSURANCE: _____
P.A./ELECT.: _____
FOOD: _____
BEVERAGES: _____
DECORATIONS: _____
PRINTING TOTALS: _____
→ TICKETS _____
→ PROGRAMME _____
POSTAGE _____
ENTERTAINMENT _____
PHOTOGRAPHER ET AL _____
MISC, _____

INCOMES:

TICKET SALES: _____
(# X EST. PRICE)
PATRONS: _____
(# X EST. PRICE)
ADS: _____
CASH BAR(?) _____
PIGGY BACK SALES: _____

CORPORATE:

TIMETABLE

APR.	MAY	JUNE	JULY	AUG.	SEPT.	OCT.
FINAL PLAN $ GOALS DECIDED	MAIL "TICKLER"					
GET CHAIRS OF SUB-COMM.						

Our committee decided to name the first event "Cleveland's Own: A Kaleidoscope of Entertainment" as a reflection of the diversity of both the people and resources of Cleveland and our neighborhood. We offered an art sale, variety show, and cocktail party at a local community arts Center. No matter how much reading and planning we did, nothing actually prepared us for successful events like experience. For example, committee women who were preparing to hang the artwork for this first event found both their adaptability and patience tested when some of the work arrived both oversized and overpriced. Further frustrations developed when the food was less than expected, and the liquor ran out! Yet from these experiences, we have learned to be more careful in choosing the caterer, and more specific in producing an art show. Our volunteers also learned valuable lessons about soliciting support, selling tickets, and budgeting both time and money. Ticket selling must be considered the number one priority. Telephone follow-up is also important. The end result? $16,000 raised for the Center, and the introduction of about 200 new people into the Center's circle.

We decided to retain the "Cleveland's Own" name for all the public events during the campaign. The second "Cleveland's Own" benefit was similar to the first. However, the committee knew how much money they wanted to raise, how to prepare more efficiently for the artwork, and how to deal more effectively with the caterer. This event introduced approximately 200 more people to the Center and netted another $16,000. We were gaining confidence and experience with each event.

The third benefit was by far our most successful. We sponsored a 'Sail-abration' at the Nautica stage in Cleveland's popular "Flats" along the Cuyahoga River. This time the Committee brainstormed ideas for a different kind of event. In keeping with the idea of "Cleveland's Own" they chose to capitalize on the popularity of clambakes in the area. The theme was nautical and music was provided by a live band. Even though the weather was threatening, the party was a smash! Our 350 person affair produced $25,000 and made the society pages!

In planning events, our committee was careful to choose ideas which reflected the Center. We are simply not a black-tie gala organization! The cocktail parties, art shows and clambake were as varied as the Center itself. Because the committee does the work, they also have

CLEVELAND'S OWN

autonomy in choosing themes which are both comfortable and feasible. Many fund raising reference books include detailed information for planning events. (See Bibliography)

HOMETOWN CLUB

The Hometown Club was the result of a brainstorming session in which we hoped to capitalize on the sentimental attachment former residents might have to the neighborhood. It was extremely difficult to locate these former residents. We sent information on this club to people on our mailing list. We put posters in churches and notices in church bulletins. We contacted Parent Teacher Associations (PTAs) and church societies. Our Speaker's Bureau publicized the Hometown Club. We attempted to get alumni lists from local schools, and discovered their reluctance to share them. We knew who our target population was, but did not know where they could be found!

Originally, we hoped to offer club-type activities, like meetings and social outings. However, few people desired those kinds of activities, and a non-meeting, monetary supporter format evolved. Now, members make a $20 donation (reduced from $50) and receive a membership card, a mug, a quarterly copy of an historical vignette, and the Center newsletter.

We set up a steering committee for this avenue whose primary function is to increase membership. A brochure describes the club and is used to recruit new members. This committee also tries to follow up on club renewals and keep membership current.

This avenue certainly has potential, but our results have been discouraging. Our original goal for the Hometown Club was $15,000 from 300 people. We have about 50 members to date, and raised $1200. We are still committed to this avenue, though we have discovered it involves a tremendous amount of time and follow-up. We are working on a series of historical vignettes about the neighborhood which represent the perspectives of former residents. We will then use these vignettes, organized into a booklet, as a donor cultivation tool, and possibly a publishable book.

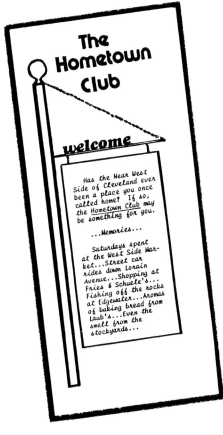

The Hometown Club

welcome

Has the Near West Side of Cleveland ever been a place you once called home? If so, the Hometown Club may be something for you.

...Memories...

Saturdays spent at the West Side Market...Street car rides down Lorain Avenue...Shopping at Fries & Schuele's... Fishing off the rocks at Edgewater...Aromas of baking bread from Laub's...Even the smell from the stockyards...

The BBC was the name given to the avenue directed toward neighborhood business donors. It served to publicize the Center and encourage local business involvement. Local business support lent credibility to our appeals to larger companies. We developed it by making visits, giving out information, inviting people to the Center for lunch and generally attempting to nurture relationships. We discovered that many local businesses were quite small, even "Mom and Pop" operations. If they could not visit, we sent literature. Sometimes a business would help us by signing bulk-mail letters or endorsing our literature to similar businesses.

The chairpersons for this avenue were people from local businesses who had already committed themselves to the Center. They hosted the business lunches and speaking engagements and tried to promote the Center whenever possible.

The BBC is really a non-group. Members share the belief that a stronger community is good for local business, and that in helping the neighborhood, they have an opportunity to expand the local workforce. Since many of the Center's programs focus on self-development for local residents, business involvement is a natural outgrowth.

Participants in the program receive a BBC decal to display at their businesses, historical highlights of the area, and the Center newsletter.

We anticipated raising $90,000 through BBC and achieved $26,612 of that goal.

ANNUAL APPEALS

Most agencies have an annual fund raising appeal, sometimes called a membership drive. It usually begins with a general mailing which asks for donations, and is followed up with phone calls, personal visits, or second letters. Our goal was $60,000. We raised $820,000 which included non-endowment direct gifts.

There is no question that a well-written letter can make a major difference in a general appeal, but careful planning of who will be appealed to, and how, are equally important. We worked from the general population to more specific target groups using our mailing list and an inverted target pyramid. (See Figure 19)

Figure 19 TARGET GROUP PYRAMID

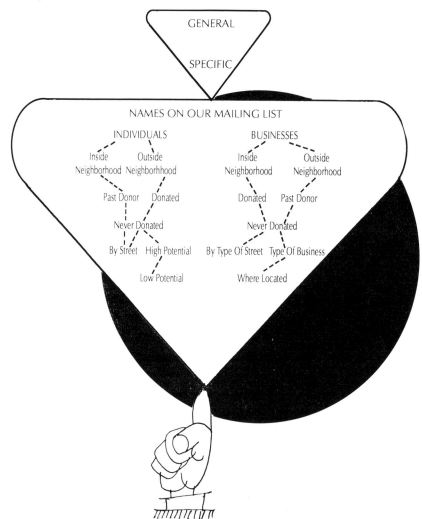

Once our specific appeal targets were selected, we focused on each one. We found that a series of letters, using different "hooks" for each targeted area and signed by someone in the target group, were very effective.

For example, a letter to medical professionals was signed by two well-known Cleveland doctors; a letter to local businesses was signed by a local business leader. Wherever possible, the letters were individually signed. We learned that people often read a post-script (P.S.), even when they haven't read the entire letter, so we tried to include a significant comment in a P.S. We also attempted to personalize our letters with handwritten notes and comments written in the margin wherever possible. The idea, of course, was to make the recipient feel special.

Another consideration was the appearance of the letter. What color paper might grab attention? What color ink to use? Should we use graphics? What salutation is most effective? The appeal letters of other agencies were good sources of ideas for us.

The appeal to neighborhood residents was first publicized by sending letters which included return envelopes. (See Figure 20). We also launched a door-to- door streetwalk, as well as follow-up phone calls. We put up banners in the building windows and, finally, held a rally. This was quite successful.

There was no real committee for this avenue, but it would have been impossible without the volunteers who spent time stuffing, labeling and mailing envelopes. We also had the assistance of volunteers with phone-a-thon and door-to-door campaigns.

When undertaking a general appeal, it is a good idea to look into the different kinds of bulk rates and postal procedures offered by the Post Office, such as buying an imprint or business reply envelopes that are paid for only when they are returned to the agency.

Figure 20 SAMPLES OF GENERAL APPEAL LETTERS

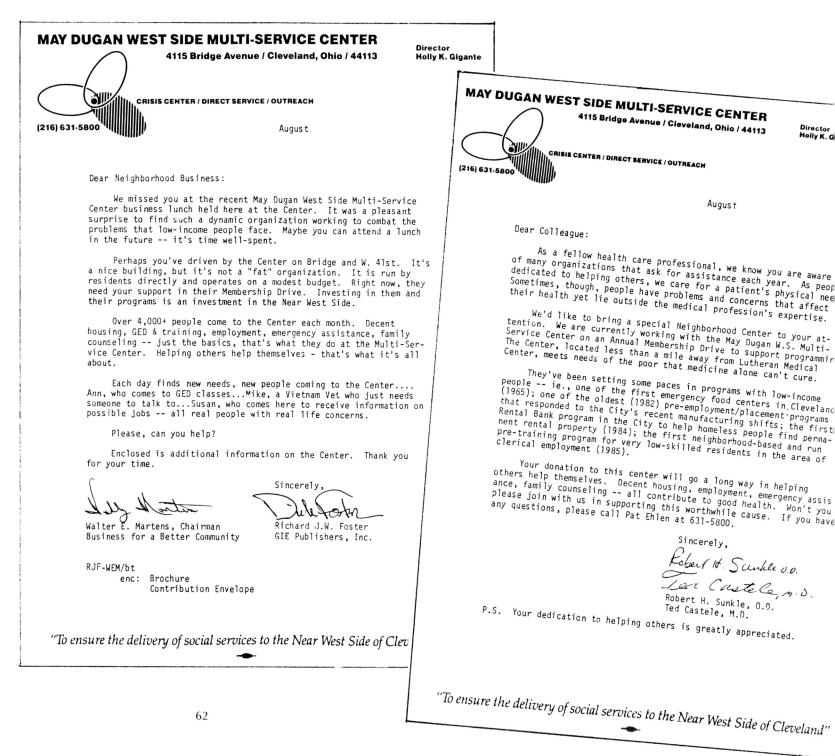

MAY DUGAN WEST SIDE MULTI-SERVICE CENTER
4115 Bridge Avenue / Cleveland, Ohio / 44113

Director
Holly K. Gigante

CRISIS CENTER / DIRECT SERVICE / OUTREACH

(216) 631-5800   August

Dear Neighborhood Business:

We missed you at the recent May Dugan West Side Multi-Service Center business lunch held here at the Center. It was a pleasant surprise to find such a dynamic organization working to combat the problems that low-income people face. Maybe you can attend a lunch in the future -- it's time well-spent.

Perhaps you've driven by the Center on Bridge and W. 41st. It's a nice building, but it's not a "fat" organization. It is run by residents directly and operates on a modest budget. Right now, they need your support in their Membership Drive. Investing in them and their programs is an investment in the Near West Side.

Over 4,000+ people come to the Center each month. Decent housing, GED & training, employment, emergency assistance, family counseling -- just the basics, that's what they do at the Multi-Service Center. Helping others help themselves - that's what it's all about.

Each day finds new needs, new people coming to the Center.... Ann, who comes to GED classes...Mike, a Vietnam Vet who just needs someone to talk to...Susan, who comes here to receive information on possible jobs -- all real people with real life concerns.

Please, can you help?

Enclosed is additional information on the Center. Thank you for your time.

Sincerely,

Walter E. Martens, Chairman
Business for a Better Community

Richard J.W. Foster
GIE Publishers, Inc.

RJF-WEM/bt
    enc: Brochure
          Contribution Envelope

"To ensure the delivery of social services to the Near West Side of Clev

62

MAY DUGAN WEST SIDE MULTI-SERVICE CENTER
4115 Bridge Avenue / Cleveland, Ohio / 44113

Director
Holly K. G

CRISIS CENTER / DIRECT SERVICE / OUTREACH

(216) 631-5800

August

Dear Colleague:

As a fellow health care professional, we know you are aware of many organizations that ask for assistance each year. As peop dedicated to helping others, we care for a patient's physical nee Sometimes, though, people have problems and concerns that affect their health yet lie outside the medical profession's expertise.

We'd like to bring a special Neighborhood Center to your attention. We are currently working with the May Dugan W.S. Multi-Service Center on an Annual Membership Drive to support programmir The Center, located less than a mile away from Lutheran Medical Center, meets needs of the poor that medicine alone can't cure.

They've been setting some paces in programs with low-income people -- ie., one of the first emergency food centers in Cleveland (1965); one of the oldest (1982) pre-employment/placement programs that responded to the City's recent manufacturing shifts; the first Rental Bank program in the City to help homeless people find permanent rental property (1984); the first neighborhood-based and run pre-training program for very low-skilled residents in the area of clerical employment (1985).

Your donation to this center will go a long way in helping others help themselves. Decent housing, employment, emergency assistance, family counseling -- all contribute to good health. Won't you please join with us in supporting this worthwhile cause. If you have any questions, please call Pat Ehlen at 631-5800.

Sincerely,

Robert H. Sunkle, O.D.
Ted Castele, M.D.

P.S. Your dedication to helping others is greatly appreciated.

"To ensure the delivery of social services to the Near West Side of Cleveland"

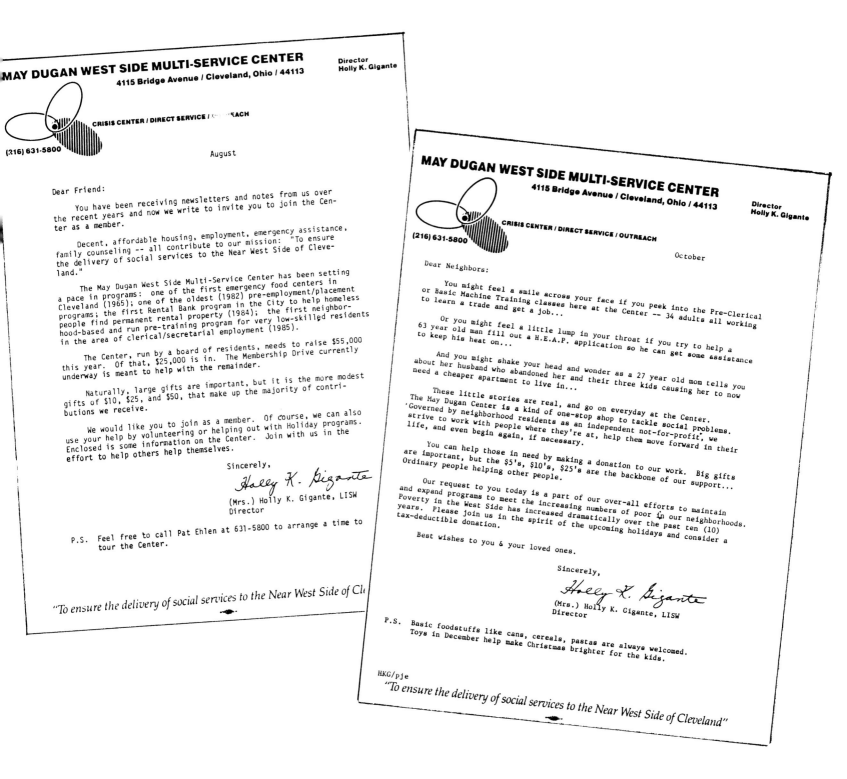

MAY DUGAN WEST SIDE MULTI-SERVICE CENTER

4115 Bridge Avenue / Cleveland, Ohio / 44113

Director
Holly K. Gigante

CRISIS CENTER / DIRECT SERVICE / OUTREACH

(216) 631-5800

August

Dear Friend:

You have been receiving newsletters and notes from us over the recent years and now we write to invite you to join the Center as a member.

Decent, affordable housing, employment, emergency assistance, family counseling -- all contribute to our mission: "To ensure the delivery of social services to the Near West Side of Cleveland."

The May Dugan West Side Multi-Service Center has been setting a pace in programs: one of the first emergency food centers in Cleveland (1965); one of the oldest (1982) pre-employment/placement programs; the first Rental Bank program in the City to help homeless people find permanent rental property (1984); the first neighborhood-based and run pre-training program for very low-skilled residents in the area of clerical/secretarial employment (1985).

The Center, run by a board of residents, needs to raise $55,000 this year. Of that, $25,000 is in. The Membership Drive currently underway is meant to help with the remainder.

Naturally, large gifts are important, but it is the more modest gifts of $10, $25, and $50, that make up the majority of contributions we receive.

We would like you to join as a member. Of course, we can also use your help by volunteering or helping out with Holiday programs. Enclosed is some information on the Center. Join with us in the effort to help others help themselves.

Sincerely,

Holly K. Gigante

(Mrs.) Holly K. Gigante, LISW
Director

P.S. Feel free to call Pat Ehlen at 631-5800 to arrange a time to tour the Center.

"To ensure the delivery of social services to the Near West Side of Cl

---

MAY DUGAN WEST SIDE MULTI-SERVICE CENTER

4115 Bridge Avenue / Cleveland, Ohio / 44113

Director
Holly K. Gigante

(216) 631-5800

CRISIS CENTER / DIRECT SERVICE / OUTREACH

October

Dear Neighbors:

You might feel a smile across your face if you peek into the Pre-Clerical or Basic Machine Training classes here at the Center -- 34 adults all working to learn a trade and get a job...

Or you might feel a little lump in your throat if you try to help a 63 year old man fill out a H.E.A.P. application so he can get some assistance to keep his heat on...

And you might shake your head and wonder as a 27 year old mom tells you about her husband who abandoned her and their three kids causing her to now need a cheaper apartment to live in...

These little stories are real, and go on everyday at the Center. The May Dugan Center is a kind of one-stop shop to tackle social problems. Governed by neighborhood residents as an independent not-for-profit, we strive to work with people where they're at, help them move forward in their life, and even begin again, if necessary.

You can help those in need by making a donation to our work. Big gifts are important, but the $5's, $10's, $25's are the backbone of our support... Ordinary people helping other people.

Our request to you today is a part of our over-all efforts to maintain and expand programs to meet the increasing numbers of poor in our neighborhoods. Poverty in the West Side has increased dramatically over the past ten (10) years. Please join us in the spirit of the upcoming holidays and consider a tax-deductible donation.

Best wishes to you & your loved ones.

Sincerely,

Holly K. Gigante

(Mrs.) Holly K. Gigante, LISW
Director

P.S. Basic foodstuffs like cans, cereals, pastas are always welcomed. Toys in December help make Christmas brighter for the kids.

HKG/pje

"To ensure the delivery of social services to the Near West Side of Cleveland"

CLUBS / BUSINESS ENDEAVORS

This avenue was intended for any additional kinds of revenue building which might evolve from our experiences during the overall campaign. We thought that a Mother's Club or a Women's Auxiliary might be formed in the future, though no new clubs have been created to date.

Business Endeavors is a new kind of fund raising technique. Non-profit agencies may produce or offer a product for sale that is directly related to the purpose of the agency. (Hospital gift shops and school bookstores are good examples.) As long as the agency is not competing with other commercial vendors in a business unrelated to its purpose, the profits are not taxable. The key is that the product must be related to the purpose of the agency.

We have sold hand-colored Mother's Day cards and t-shirts under this plan. As we continue to write our historical vignettes through the Hometown Club avenue, we might publish and sell them.

We have not invested much time in this avenue, so we have not raised our $10,000 goal. We have raised $ 1,540 . It is a potential source of revenue that deserves more attention.

CAPITAL IMPROVEMENTS

"Bricks and mortar" money is an ongoing need. Since we were undertaking a major fund raising campaign, it made sense to include an avenue for capital improvements in our original plans. We looked at our physical plant and dreamed a little about potential needs. The building, for example, is 15 years old, and we considered possible maintenance work. We wanted to expand our parking lot, and since the building is occupied to capacity, anticipated a possible addition. We also needed storage space. Without a really clear picture of our needs, we estimated some costs and came up with a goal of over $374,000 for this avenue. Capital improvements are attractive to the donor who likes to be able to "see" what he has donated.

However, we did not allow enough planning time before we began to raise money. The Board tried to determine where we would get the land. Did we want to destroy residential property to increase our parking lot? If we were going to expand the building, how and where were we going to do it? We had ballpark figures for our improvements, but not the technical specifications. By the time we realized that we needed architectural designs, land costs, and other data, we were already knee-deep in the campaign. Because of our lack of planning, we had no real committee for this avenue. Members of the Advisory Cabinet made contacts with people they knew who would support capital improvements, but those contacts were used for smaller needs, not expansion.

We did have some donors targeted for this avenue. We went through lists of companies and foundations looking for those which frequently supported capital improvement campaigns. We wrote some proposals, but found that many national foundations and companies prefer to give to larger capital improvements and expect name recognition in return.

Our goal for Capital Improvements was $374,000; we reached $17,875 ($6,275 from '87). The important thing about this avenue is that we found donors who could be solicited in future capital efforts. And, we will probably focus on capital needs as a separate campaign which includes maintenance and operations costs as secondary focus .

Chapter 6
DEVELOPING OUR RESOURCES

*W*hy do people give? There are dozens of reasons. It often has to do with the kind of person one is, the kind of commitments one makes. Some people need to feel important. Some come in touch with their own humanity by touching others. Each is different, or may change along the way. Seldom is a person encountered who does not want to eliminate pain or suffering in some way. We are all human beings and seem to relate to human causes and needs. It is the job of the social agency to provide opportunities to both those who wish to help and those who need help. This concept is an important building block in developing resources.

Who gives money to agencies like the May Dugan Center? Once we recognized the need to promote ourselves, the question arose, "to whom?" Supporters can be men or women, the old or the young, school children or college students, professionals and non-professionals, people who live in the neighborhood and those who do not, churches, businesses, and other agencies. The diversity of potential supporters is overwhelming; the trick is identifying them!

Once potential groups are identified, it is possible to name specific supporters. For example, we knew the names of twenty churches in our neighborhood. Knowing who we'd like to give us money, and who might give us money was the first step. Knowing how

67

to approach them was the second. We needed to learn what might appeal to specific individuals and groups, as well as who was the best person to deliver our request. Just as one personally develops a circle of friends, so did the Center.

In an attempt to get the support of individuals, we had a Public Appeals avenue (see Chapter 5, The "People Helping People" Campaign) which used direct mail and phone calls. Within this avenue, we divided potential supporters into those who never heard of us, and those who knew us but never gave. We tried to make personal contact with those who already knew us.

We asked schools to have canned food drives or pasta days. In an effort to get children and parents involved with the Center, we offered to provide speakers to classes and the PTA to talk about problems in the neighborhood.

Often, a letter was a good approach. For example, our Hometown Club appealed to graduates of a local high school with a letter signed by a fellow alumnus. Follow-up phone calls built on the "old school ties," and often the personal, one-on-one encounter resulted in a new donation. In a similar way, the local person who "sold" the Center to his or her neighbors generated new support. People trust their friends, and gifts of various sizes were given to us because of the approach of one person to another.

This one-to-one, someone-who-knows-someone approach was certainly essential for large donations. The CEO who discussed his commitment to the Center with a friend often got us a donation. People who were involved with the Center invited business associates to visit us. There was nothing that worked better in obtaining big gifts than to arrange a tour of the building for potential donors. Letters and phone calls were fine introductions, but when people visited the Center, it literally sold itself. Of those who visited, 90% contributed!

Often people wanted to become involved in ways other than, or in addition to, monetary contributions. These included selling tickets, or packing food; or offering a gift-in-kind, such as a nursery owner who would give flowers, or a person who would give us a computer. It was important to have a "TO DO" list of projects or a "WISH LIST" of needs so that we could tell a person in what special and particular ways she/he could help. (See Figure 21)

Figure 21 WISH LIST AND "TO DO" LIST

WISH LIST

Camera   Folding chairs
VCR/TV   Lobby Furniture
Diapers/Paper Products   Non-perishable items
Flag   Kitchen utensils
Caramate slide projector   Wall clock
Room Dividers   Kids books
Chalk Board Cleaning items
Public Address System
Paint

TO DO LIST

Pack Food Bags
Chair Public Relations Committee
Solicit prospects for donations
Filing
Data-Entry
Follow-up phone calls to clients
Research prospects at Foundation Library
Write thank you letters
Write a historical vignette for HTC
Chaperone a Youth Activity
Pick up food donations
Prepare lunch for visiting business group
Help with a Phone-athon
Go house hunting with Staff

We developed a Volunteer Manual containing a list of jobs. We then learned about specific donors, talking about their interests, and tried to match them to a job which will be enjoyed and not result in boredom or failure. In this way we entrusted him or her with part of our work, making the donor feel needed and appreciated. We also were ready with a cost list for a variety of needs and activities ranging from $25 to

$20,000. The range was wide so that anyone who wanted to donate could afford to do so. For example, a donation of $50 kept the building open for one night. We needed a new TV and VCR, a public address system, paint for the community room, or an additional staff person for a specific project. Whatever a donor might be in a position to give us — money, time, service — could be readily integrated with our needs.

As we learned about our supporters, we recognized that there were some who wanted to make a "one-shot" donation. For those people, the capital improvement avenue was the most attractive. Another type of "one-shot" contribution is a planned gift. It is very difficult to start a planned giving program, and any kind of planned giving calls for a long term commitment on the part of the donor, but it does represent a "one-shot" gift, rather than a pledge over time.

In developing donor relations it is important to represent the agency in the best possible light, but as it really is. Our organization is not flashy and we don't need to appear flashy. We built on the strengths of who we are and what we do. Our strongest selling point is our belief in the people we serve.

To summarize, we learned that developing our resources resulted from: 1) identifying groups of donors; 2) matching those groups to appropriate fund raising avenues; 3) naming as many specific donors as possible; 4) brainstorming about our financial needs; 5) using the most effective "asking" approach for each potential donor, (see Chapter 7, The "Ask"); and 6) involving people as volunteers as well as donors.

It all makes good sense.

Friendly entrance of the May Dugan Center

Chapter 7
THE "ASK"

*A*sking for money is extremely difficult. From the time we are children, we associate asking for money with being unable to support ourselves. While most agencies work to be self-sufficient, it is seldom possible. So, we must ask for money. We have learned some tricks of the trade during this campaign which have made asking for funds, if not easier, more productive.

There are mountains of books, workshops, and resources available to agencies on this topic (See Bibliography). We studied our books and asked questions of successful fund raisers, learning from the experience of others and applying their knowledge to our situation.

We established four simple techniques which we kept in mind whenever we asked for money. These were applicable to all asking situations, from the door-to-door campaign to the major donation:

1. Ask for a specific amount. Do not say, "Please donate." Instead, state an amount. "If you donate $5 to the Center, you will provide food for a family for two days." "Your contribution of $2,700 will purchase 12 new electric type-writers to be used in our re-training program." "You can support our Employment Services for two years with a contribution of $50,000." Whatever the situation, a specific amount provides a starting point.

2. Know what buys what. Put dollar figures on services. A $70 donation may cover the monthly cost of the phone lines used in the job placement program. This works together with the idea of asking for a specific amount. People want to get something for their money. Show them what their contribution can do.

3. Ask for the money in a comfortable situation. The wealthy should ask the wealthy. The poor should ask the poor. A neighborhood resident will not be effective in getting a donation from a wealthy executive; he or she may not even be able to get in the door. The social chasm is too great, and the situation too uncomfortable for both parties. If, however, a business associate phones a friend and suggests that he make a donation to a worthy cause, there is a greater possibility of success. If a local resident knocks on the door of a neighbor and endorses the work of the Center, he is much more likely to get a donation.

4. Know whom we're asking money for. In asking for money, we must be able to describe the people we serve. A case statement is a short story which describes who benefits from contributions. A young mother who comes to the Center seeking milk for her baby presents a heart-tugging picture. Being able to provide her not only with milk, but with job training and placement confirms the value of the donation. (See Figure 22)

Figure 22 SAMPLE CASE STATEMENTS

Patricia J.Ehlen

October

Sample

So many faces, so many cultures, young and old alike - all with a common bond - they are the poor, the disadvantaged - 60% of the population on the Near West Side. 4000+ each month, poor yet proud, they come to the May Dugan West Side Multi-Service Center for help - they come here to find a way to better their lives.

Mary Jo is 40, a widow on welfare trying to raise three kids. Her husband died unexpectedly last year - she was left penniless and lacked a high school education. She came in last month for help. Scared and anxious she began to work with a counselor to sort out her troubles. She's taken a first step to resolving some problems by starting high school classes here at the Center.

Then there's Juan who's looking for a job. He came in to receive job counseling and check our job postings for a position.

Jane came in to find a new place to live. Jane and her three kids are scared and she wants to find a safe place for them to live.

Inez, who at 70 is lonely and gets confused with the changes she encounters in life comes to sit for awhile and find answers to her problems .

All real people...with real problems.
All they need is someone to "lend a hand" - that is what we try to do here at the May Dugan West Side Multi-Services Center - the only independent self-help, multi-service center left on the West Side.

By offering services such as personal and family counseling, rental assistance, General Education Diploma classes, pre-clerical training, job counseling, crisis intervention and referral, and emergency food distribution, people can really find help.

All real people with real problems. Nothing fancy - just the basics.

Won't you help to raise $20,000 to keep programs going? Help us help others - encourage people to take the first step by reaching out. We need you! With your help we can increase our services, expand our involvement in the neighbrhood and really make a difference.

Sample

'NEIGHBORS PULLING TOGETHER IN A LOW-INCOME COMMUNITY TO
RESOLVE THEIR PROBLEMS OF HUNGER , DECENT HOUSING, JOB ACCESS,
FEAR OF CRIME, COMMERCIAL STABILITY"...
makes for great headlines in any northern urban city; but here on
W.41st and Bridge in Cleveland's west side, neighbors do just that.
Developed over 10 years ago by residents who wanted to provide
social services to the community and help low-income neighbors help
themselves, the West Side Multi-Service / Crisis Center remains
a hub of aid to this multi-cultural neighborhood. Here, men, women
and youth find a dependable source of information, counsel and
outreach in various social issues that affect them . They often
put back into the Center volunteer assistance by which they also
gain new skills and dignity. Because of recent cuts in government
funds for programs it is necessary to raise $60,000 to maintain
current services. With this assistance, low-income people can
continue to solve today's problems and to prepare themselves and
their families for the furure.

Asking In A General Appeal

All four asking techniques were used in a general appeal letter. We found that we could pull certain categories of potential donors from our mailing list. A separate "hook" or lead, or case statement applied to each category. For example, a letter to local businesses asked for a $100 donation to the job training program so that 40 participants could attend classes for one week. The letter was signed by a Center supporter who owned or worked at a local business. It also included a personal note written in the margin or a post script from a Center committee member who was actually acquainted with the letter's recipient.

The letter (See Figure 20, Chapter 5) also noted that the gift is tax deductible, and listed any premium which might be given for a donation, i.e. a membership card, a decal, a mug, etc. A return envelope, stamped with the Center's address was included.

A follow-up person contacted letter recipients either by phone or with another letter. It was extremely important to send a thank you note and keep a record of all donations.

Asking Through Speaking Engagements

Originally, our Speaker's Bureau developed as we knocked on doors in an effort to get the word out about the Center. It has become quite successful in its own right and we now receive frequent requests to send speakers to a variety of local organizations. Whenever we made a presentation, we used the four asking techniques, plus a few extras.

When addressing a group, we always sent around a sign-up sheet, asking for the names and addresses of those in attendance. We then added these names to our mailing list.

We spoke about the Center, describing our services in terms of those we assist: a verbal presentation of our case statement, and a way to show people what we do. We sometimes brought our homemade slide show.

We entertained questions and tried our very best to answer them. We used the opportunity to note that donations are always welcome, pointing out that donations of $5 and $10 are the backbone of support for many programs. We would comment that $5 goes a long way at the food bank or that $35 keeps the phone lines working for two weeks. We brought literature on the Center, and left a stack of self-addressed, unstamped envelopes for potential gifts.

Asking for Direct Gifts (Large)

Asking for big gifts required the four basic techniques plus knowledge about the prospect, a sense of timing, and some intuition. While the asking was the same, the situation was different.

Asking for a big gift was usually a one-to-one situation. We asked either an individual, or a representative of a group, but we asked for large gifts only from those we knew were in a position to give them. For example, if we hoped to get $50,000 over two years for training programs from a corporate foundation, the first thing we would do is make certain that this foundation supported training programs.

The second step would be to invite the Foundation's representative to visit the Center. Once at the Center, we would present our case. Visiting the Center was the best way to elicit support, but if that was impossible we would go to the donor armed with literature about the Center. The "we" always included both staff and the Cabinet or Board member(s) who set up the contact.

77

Once the case had been made, we would ask for the specific amount, in this case $50,000 and then be quiet. It was important to allow the prospective donor to think about our request, so silence was golden. Many fund raisers say, "the first person who speaks after the 'ask' usually loses."

In the best of all scenarios, the donor said a resounding "Yes, of course!" wrote us a check, and we all left happy. But that was not the normal course of events. Perhaps the reaction was less than positive, or the amount was too high. Then it was time to negotiate. This is the area where timing and intuition were invaluable. If the donor offered to donate part of the requested sum, we took it! It was often necessary to write a follow-up proposal for a large sum. If so, we wrote the proposal with an attached budget and a cover letter from both the solicitor and a separate supportive person and mailed the entire package to the prospective donor. In all cases, being prepared to provide facts, figures and projected results was vital to achieving success.

Asking For Gifts (Small)

Whenever we launched a door-to-door campaign, either for local businesses or residences, we tried to train our solicitors to use the four basic techniques in their approaches.

We usually wrote out a speech for them which included the specific amount, what it would buy and who will be served by it. We also tried to teach solicitors to be appreciative of any donations, and the importance of presenting a positive face and winning friends for the Center.

If we were calling on local businesses, for example, and the business person was reluctant to donate, we might invite him or her to the Center to see what we do, or perhaps to one of our business luncheons.

If a person was at the Center, the same rules applied. Often we found that people began by making donations of food or clothing or items for a garage sale. It was important to recognize that they were good candidates to take the next step and make a monetary gift, but they needed to be asked. If intuition told the solicitor to ask for a specific item, like a flagpole from the Kiwanis Club, we did it. We also asked for things like printing, paint, typewriters, and an alarm system.

While asking for money may not be easy, it is the very heart of providing the services needed in our community. We learned that the "how" of asking was as important as the "how much".

Chapter 8
IN
THE
NEWS

*W*e knew from the beginning that public relations would be the under-girding of our fund raising success. We had stressed public relations in our original proposal to the Cleveland Foundation. (See Figure 23, page 82)

We also knew that there was a tremendous amount of competition for media attention and that the May Dugan Center did not present the flashy, sensational kind of items that usually draw interest.

As with most other aspects of this campaign, we began with our "inner circle" of supporters. Our early news releases were met with indifference, our radio and TV coverage was practically non-existent, but our word-of-mouth, one-on-one, let- me-tell-you-about-the-Center grape-vine worked overtime! And while our diligent supporters went about spreading our name, we gained experience in dealing with the media.

81

Figure 23 THREE YEAR TIMETABLE

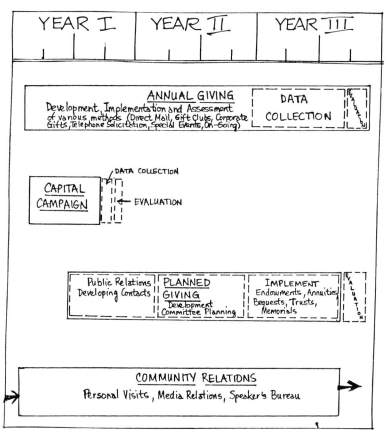

We learned to read the newspapers and watch the TV. We tried to stay current with local news in case there was a way we could "piggyback" on a publicized story. For example, if a news story discussed local vocational education, we called immediately to mention our pre-clerical training program.

We also learned to have a Press Kit handy. A Press Kit contains flyers, brochures, and background information on the Center, and introduces the agency to media, TV, radio, and print. It is supplemented by news releases. Some agencies have glossy, expensively prepared press kits, but ours was pretty simple. We tried to choose information that was not "pat" or "bleeding heart", yet conveyed the nature of our services.

Another important resource is a Media Guide. This directory contains the names of the contact people at all the local television and radio stations and newspapers. It also gives advice on how to write Public Service Announcements and Press Releases. We purchased the Media Guide annually and then sent or hand-delivered copies of our Press Kit to the contact people.

We wrote Letters to the Editor on relevant issues, and had some success getting them printed, and we sent copy to the Op-ed section of the newspaper.

We continuously took black and white photographs of people, events, and activities at the Center, in close-ups and group shots of people at work. We had legal releases signed by those who appeared in the photographs, so that we could use them with news releases, in our annual reports, or on display boards used by our Speakers Bureau. We also made certain to have our events listed on the Community Calendars sponsored by the City Club and Junior League. This way we avoided dates that conflicted with other organizations, as well as made our name known.

With all this effort, it has taken us almost three full years to develop name recognition. We have received more coverage from the weekly community papers than from the daily Cleveland Plain Dealer, in part because we have been lucky enough to catch the interest of a local reporter, but even The Plain Dealer is giving us more ink (see Figure 24, pages 84-89). The newspapers are more likely to cover our public events, like the Cleveland's Own benefits, than to print our news releases, so we have to urge society reporters to mention our programs in their stories about the parties.

Developing media exposure takes a tremendous amount of time and work. We have learned to be relentless in getting our name out, but all our public relations successes began with the efforts of our loyal supporters. The bottom line is, if your story gets media coverage it will reach a broad base of people, but to really gain new supporters and reach the people with highest potential of helping your agency, the grapevine is the way to go. In the long run, the grapevine will reach more people, more often, and in a more personal manner making it more effective for the small agency.

Church reaches out, shelters homeless

By MICHAEL O'MALLEY
STAFF WRITER

Members of the Parma Lutheran Church congregation are not satisfied with simply reflecting on the teachings of Christ. They have taken their Christian beliefs to the streets — where the homeless live.

The church's Community Ministry Committee has established a **Parma** program that pays security deposits and up to six months' rent for selected homeless families.

Since 1988, when the program began, the church has spent more than $8,000 to shelter nine families.

"Too many times we're concerned with our own material gains and we're not concerned with other people," said Ruth Berzins, a co-chairman of the committee. "We just feel it's part of our Christian outreach if we can help the homeless. Any one of us could be in that situation. I think we should share.

"When you are helping the poor you are actually helping God," Berzins added, quoting the words of Christ as interpreted by the New Testament evangelist Matthew: "Truly I say to you, as you did it to one of the least of these my brethren, you did it to me."

A newspaper article on the May Dugan Center, a non-profit social service agency helping the poor and homeless on Cleveland's near West Side, was brought to the attention of the church committee in 1987.

The following year, church members adopted their first homeless family' through the agency "and they have been doing it ever since," said Lillian LaBoy of the center. "Right now, we're working on the 10th family."

LaBoy said she screens 80 to 100 homeless families a month for rental assistance from the agency, and out of that number she chooses one.

"We just don't want to give out money," LaBoy said. "We want to choose a family that wants to make it, that just needs a helping hand."

She said homeless people who are mentally ill or drug abusers would not qualify for the agency's rental assistance because there are other programs for them.

Among those families helped by Parma Lutheran are a woman who fled from her physically abusive husband, taking her two young children with her, and a man who lost his job because of illness and eventually lost his home.

"Without our help they would be out on the street," Berzins said, noting that helping only nine disadvantaged families may not be significant when hundreds are without shelter.

"But if everybody would do a small part, that would help the entire situation."

Though the church is willing to pay rents for up to six months, the families it has helped have not needed that amount of assistance and have been able to support themselves after three or four months.

Parma Lutheran has stipulated that it help the needy families without them knowing where the money comes from.

"They know there's a church, but they don't know where it is," LaBoy said. "These people have pride. We don't want the families to feel they owe people something."

Berzins said the families were not required to pay back the rent money but they are asked to pay back the rental deposit under any payment plan that they can afford.

"It gives them the feeling that the money they're returning is helping others," Berzins said. "We don't know the people. We've never met them. But we know they're grateful."

As the church prepares to help its 10th family, LaBoy's business of sheltering homeless families is entering its peak season.

"Christmas happens to be a bi season for evictions because peopl want to buy toys for their kids, an they don't pay the rent," LaBo said.

METRO WATCH

Poor offered veterinary care for their pets

A Free Animal Clinic Team will be at the May Dugan West Side Multi-Service Center, 4115 Bridge Ave., from 2 to 4 p.m. Wednesday. Dogs, cats and other pets of low-income residents will be examined and treated free by a veterinarian. People are asked to bring their welfare or medical cards as identification.

May Dugan Center plans yard sale Sept. 7

The May Dugan Multi-Service Center, 4115 Bridge Ave., will have a yard sale Sept. 7 from 9 a.m. to 4 p.m. on its front lawn. Items include household goods, collectibles, jewelry, books and toys. The center provides job counseling and training, crisis intervention, personal and family counseling, housing assistance, emergency food, youth work information and referral.

West Side center plans two job training programs

Two entry-level job training programs will begin in the next several weeks at the May Dugan West Side Multi-Service Center. Space is limited and interested people should apply now, the center said.

The programs are open to those 18 or older. No G.E.D. or high school diploma is required.

A Pre-Clerical Training program will begin Sept. 17 and run for nine months. The program, offered in coordination with Cuyahoga Community College, consists of basic math and English, speech, typing, filing and office procedures.

Financial assistance for low-income participants is usually available.

The second program, Basic Machine Training, begins Oct. 1 and runs for six months. Classes are offered in blueprint reading, machine theory, basic math and English. There also is hands-on experience on actual machines.

The program is offered in coordination with the Cleveland Public Schools' office of adult and continuing education.

The May Dugan Center, at 4115 Bridge Ave., also offers support services such as job counseling and job placement. For more information, call 631-5800.

PD photos/RAMON OWENS

Sandy Sullivan of Fairview Park, a benefit adviser, looks especially nautical as she congratulates her son, Sean Sullivan, on his seafood. Sullivan is president of Navillus Gourmet Fish Co. If you look closely, Navillus is Sullivan spelled backwards.

Maudie Holm and her husband, Otto Holm Jr. of Cleveland, look over the "Sail-abration" program.

From left, Mary Sullivan of Rocky River, co-chairwoman of "Sail-abration"; Pat Ehlen of Parma Heights, and Susan Grimberg of Lakewood, who is Sullivan's sister and was co-chairwoman.

A 'Sail-abration'

Three hundred eighty supporters of the May Dugan Multi-Service Center turned out for the center's biggest fund-raiser to date, called "Sail-abration," Sept. 29 at the Nautica Stage in the Fla...

Though the weather "outside" wasn't ... delightful, everybody had a good time in ... tents set up on the stage. There was no s... was lots of 'bration as partygoers enjoye... featuring Navillus Gourmet Seafood and ... Impacto Nuevo band.

Benefit planners raised $25,000 for the ... 4115 Bridge Ave. It helps residents improv... and break the cycle of poverty.

SUN PHOTOS BY JEFF FARR

Mary Caldwell, president of the May Dugan Board of Trustees, and Tom Sullivan, campaign chairman, were all smiles Saturday night at the clam bake, where enough "clams" were shelled out by the guests to do a lot of good for center programs.

Cleveland's hot band, Impacto Nuevo.

Figure 24

COVERAGE FROM THE MEDIA

ARTS&LIVING

D

West Side's one-stop social services center

Sharon Campbell and her children, Alberto, 2 months, and Ra[...] at the multi-service center to make sure they got a bag of food[...] 150 neighborhood families a month.

By NORINE DWORKIN
STAFF WRITER

Mary Alston has 26 cents in her pocket, a dollar in the bank.

She can't carry all she owns in her two gym bags, but she doesn't trust the transients at the shelter where she's sleeping. She says they steal.

She's been in two shelters since she lost her home in July. Now she beds down at the West Side Catholic Center, but it allows transients to stay no more than 10 days. She's got eight days left, and she's running out of options.

She's hoping that the West Side Multi-Service Center can help her find a job.

Alston is just one of more than 3,000 jobless, homeless and uneducated people who come through the doors of the May Dugan West Side Multi-Service Center every month looking for help.

The multi-service center, born of the War on Poverty, straddles the corner of Bridge and W. 41st Sts. Although about 40% Hispanic, it is a neighborhood of such ethnic diversity that one volunteer dubbed the center's clientele a "Heinz 57 mix."

There is to fill the basic needs of survival — to help with job or home loss, hunger, smooth family squabbles — the staff offers advice on everything from utility bills to broken hot water heaters, said Phyllis Hager, a human services worker.

It's a walk-in facility, something staff members pride themselves on. If the situation is desperate, one can always find a sympathetic ear; the staff listens even when it's not so desperate. No one leaves without help.

The yearly budget of $261,178

covers eight core services, which include a crisis center, emergency food distribution, rent and job banks. The center generates most of its revenues from rents collected from other agencies that use the building and fund-raisers. It also receives state and county funding as well as occasional grants from foundations such as the Cleveland Foundation.

Before Alston left the building, she had leads on two low-cost efficiencies and an appointment with Bill Winans, the employment director.

"People have really been helping me," said Alston. "I went a long time without help. I didn't know there was so much."

"If they can't help you directly, they'll find someone who can," said VISTA volunteer Aida Perez.

The staff works hard instilling self-confidence in the clients. Morale-lifters dot the hallways, encouraging clients to feel good about themselves and be independent.

Approximately 150 families receive monthly food baskets, but recipients are encouraged to return for self-reliance seminars on such topics as freezing food or urban gardening.

The center is not to be used as a crutch, said Winans. "Empowering people to do their own job search rather than have them depend on us for openings, that's more of what I want to see."

In his cubicle, Winans counsels Tom Roman of Cleveland on interview etiquette. Just out of the Marines, Roman is applying for a shipping-and-receiving position at Hollenden House.

"Hotels are very particular about appearance," Winans cautions Roman, clad in a T-shirt and fati-

gues. "If you go in as you are now, they won't consider you."

Before Roman leaves, Winans also attaches a paper clip to the referral form so Roman won't forget to attach it to the application. That referral is a seal of approval from the center, an approval that often is chancy.

"It's risky to meet people and that same day refer them," admits Winans, who knows that weak referrals can damage the center's reputation.

Sometimes a match is made and sometimes not. Last week an employer, walking in off the street, hired a client right out of Winans' cubicle.

It's all about helping yourself.

That's how Aida Perez and Carla Murico work. In their "pre-clerical" training classes, they teach low-income, jobless women much more than typing and eighth-grade math.

"(Some) women are afraid to leave their homes," said Perez.

"It's a fear," added Murico. "We get a lot of women who haven't worked. They've been to the grocery store and to friends' houses. We get them used to taking classes."

Murico and Perez do all they can to make sure their students get to class. They pick them up when their cars break down, assist with day care and accompany the women who are too advanced for the pre-clerical program to Cuyahoga Community College to enroll in other classes.

If they enroll enough students, CCC will send over two instructors. That doesn't look possible this year, said Murico. Besides, what they could really use are some typewriters that work.

Perez, 34, tells the women who

come [...]
Divorce[...]
still ma[...]
and vol[...]
she c[...]
same. [...]

"It's [...]
'I don't[...]

The [...]
grams [...]
rent s[...]
West [...]
30-pa[...]
Side [...]
betwe[...]
ity i[...]
the [...]

Th[...]
inde[...]
such[...]
Side[...]
cei[...]
ter[...]
ind[...]
the[...]
for[...]
an[...]
ou[...]
te[...]
S[...]
e[...]
l[...]

Crain's Cleveland Business

140 Public Square, Suite 404, Cleveland OH 44114 (216) 522-1383

Brian D. Tucker
Editor / associate publisher

Crain's Cleveland Business.

OPINION

Editorials

Keep giving

Donating money and time has long been a part of corporate Cleveland. Executives who move here to take top-level jobs sometimes are taken aback by the culture they encounter. It is simply expected that volunteer work will be part of his or her job. A pioneer United Way city, Cleveland is a leader in the nation each year in per-capita giving. Much of that is engineered by executives at Cleveland-area firms, including the publisher of this newspaper.

Thus it is with regret that we watch the shrinkage of some locally based corporations' charity budgets (see story and list, page 13). BP Amerca Inc., the Cleveland area's largest corporate giver, has cut its budget by $6 million since 1985. More than half of the 35 companies on our list trimmed their donations in the most recently reported year. And that is not a local phenomenon. A New York-based trade group that tracks corporate philanthropy nationwide said giving had dropped $100 million in the past year.

That worries people like Holly Gigante, the energetic director of the May Dugan West Side Multi-Service Center. Her organization, which serves a population of 100,000 in Ohio City and adjacent near-West Side neighborhoods, leaves few stones unturned in the search for operating funds. In addition to seeking grants for the job placement and clerical training provided there, the center also acts as a landlord, renting office space to various organizations serving the local population.

And this center is not a welfare operation; the staff follows a philosophy of truly helping people help themselves. "If they need clerical training, we'll help them with their skills enough that they can get into a more advanced training program," the director said. "We tell them how they should go about getting and going to a job interview ... what the employers expect. Then they have to go and apply for jobs themselves." That effort was given a big boost recently when a typewriter company donated new electric models for the center's classroom.

These people care deeply about their mission, and they know that Cleveland-area companies are run by people who understand what poverty means to the entire local economy. Like RPM Inc. chairman Thomas Sullivan, who heads the center's advisory committee. He gets nothing for his company, which is headquartered in Medina. But helping that neighborhood helps all of us.

That's the feeling of most executives at Cleveland-area firms. We just hope that it continues to be reflected in their donations. It's one of the things that makes this community special.

May Dugan's helping spirit lives on

By JULIE SOWA
Staff Writer

In the 1930s and '40s, May Dugan was a bartender on the Near West Side who, out of the goodness of her heart, served up food and advice to her poor neighbors.

In the 1970s and '80s, the May Dugan Multi-Service Center on Bridge Avenue in Ohio City is an example of people helping people and a model for centers across the nation.

The center is kn the midst of celebrating its 20th birthday.

"MAY DUGAN DID A LOT for the little people of the community," said Holly Gigante, a Lakewood resident who has served as director of the center for eight years.

"There's a lot of people who do a lot for others and never get any credit for it," she added. "For example, those who are taking care of an ill family member."

Staffers and volunteers from all over the west side have witnessed many such heroic real-life dramas being played out over the years. Advisory cabinet member Sandra Sullivan of Fairview Park is one volunteer who has a lot of respect for the people served by the center.

"The poor have a lot of tenacity — I guess you could call it courage," she said. "They share a lot of themselves. They don't have a lot but they'll share it."

Gigante added, "They don't think they are courageous, though. Maybe that's the hero in them."

Both women agreed that a major reason people come to the center is to create a better life for their children. "All mothers throughout time have wanted a better life for their children," said Sullivan.

THE CENTER first opened its doors as the May Dugan West Side Multi-Service Center on Lorain Avenue in 1965. It was based on the War on Poverty concept, developed by President John F. Kennedy, which held that poor people are best suited to solve their own problems.

People from the neighborhood were the ones who planned the center when it was incorporated as the Near West Side Multi-Service Corporation in 1969.

When the new 32,000-square-foot facility was built in 1975 on the site of the former Lourdes Academy, May Dugan's name was tacked back on. Dugan died in the early '70s.

Near West Side residents still play an important role in keeping the center going. Fifty percent of the volunteers are from the neighborhoods and 50 percent are from far-

ther west, said Gigante. Last year, 185 people volunteered at the center.

"Without volunteers there'd be no way we could provide services," said Phillis Hager, a paid staff member who started out as a volunteer, and in fact, still volunteers.

"People who come for food will often end up as volunteers or contributors," she said.

For example, during the last teachers' strike, some teachers had to avail themselves of the services offered at the center. Now two of those teachers take it upon themselves to send $100 to the center each month, Hager said.

SERVICES PROVIDED at the center could fill a book. Just about every need imaginable is seen to, except those provided by other, nearby agencies. But all services promote self-help.

"We don't just hand out food," said Patricia Ehlen, resource developer. "They have to take nutrition classes."

There are also classes on things such as how to budget money and how to control rodent problems in the home.

Hager is in charge of basic human services at the center, as well as the Homemakers Club, where residents can make friends and learn money-saving ideas. The center has served 1,350 families so far this year, and about 4,000 people a month, she said.

A citizens group headed by Ethel Jennings lends itself to community involvement. At the moment, the group is working on getting the Cleveland public schools to open school buildings in the evenings to keep children off the streets.

Teens and pre-teens are of special concern at the May Dugan center. Last summer, the "Teen Forum," composed of young people ages 14-18, published its own magazine containing inspirational writings. This summer, a new pre-teen group was formed for ages 10-13.

The idea behind both groups is to provide constructive opportunities to learn good citizenship, Gigante said.

Inspiring motivation in clients is the main job of counselor Karin Heller.

"Drugs are not always the problem," Ehlen said, adding that people caught up in the poverty cycle may have a hard time climbing out of the rut.

As far as employment counseling is concerned, the center goes be-

SUN PHOTOS BY JOE DA...
...es the many services offered
...d by Lillian LaBoy.

THURSDAY JULY 20.

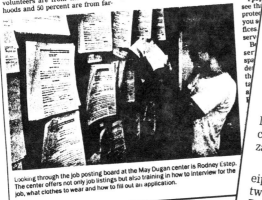

Looking through the job posting board at the May Dugan center is Rodney Estep. The center offers not only job listings but also training in how to interview for the job, what clothes to wear and how to fill out an application.

87

Center gets $30,000 from feds

W.S. SUN NEWS

A federal matching grant of up to $30,000 to support evening instruction programs has been awarded to the May Dugan West Side Multi-Service Center, 4115 Bridge Ave.

Patricia Ehlen, resource developer at the center, said the Department of Housing and Urban Development grant will match the center's fund-raising efforts this year on a 4-to-1 ratio. The center hopes to raise $7,500 with the aid of volunteers, she said.

Some 2,500 families benefit from the center's programs, Ehlen said.

Holly Gigante, center director, said support in raising money is being sought from both residents and businessess.

"We believe in helping people help themselves," she said. "This matching grant has the same philosophy and gives both responsibility and support to neighborhood self-help."

The center offers evening programs in adult basic education toward obtaining a high school equivalency diploma, in English as a second language, in typing and more.

It also offers help in applying for home weatherization programs and low-interest housing rehab loans, and holds regular meetings on issues of community concern, such as homelessness, safety and commercial revitalization.

Ehlen said about 50 volunteers are helping to raise money to assure receipt of the matching grant funds. The money must be raised in the area between the Cuyahoga River to West 85th Street and from Lake Erie to Denison Avenue.

LENDING A HAND

SUN PHOTO BY JOE GLICK

As training coordinator at May Dugan West Side Multi-Service Center on Bridge Avenue, Reid Proctor spends a lot of time in the typing room. The center, which is celebrating its 20th birthday, was organized by and still gets most of its input from neighboring residents. For more about the center, see page C1.

For more about the center, see page C1.

METRO WATCH

Center workshops to focus on women's health

May Dugan West Side Multi-Service Center, 4115 Bridge Ave., will observe Women's Health Month with four free public workshops. The topics and times include health screening, Thursday, 9 a.m. to noon; drug awareness, Thursday, 1:15 to 3:30 p.m.; weight management, Friday 10 a.m. to noon, and safe dating, Friday 4 to 6 p.m. Call Reid Proctor or Lillian LaBoy, 631-5800, for more information.

JULIE'S JOTTINGS
JULIE SOWA

HONORING ACHIEVEMENT — Last week 16 students met in the lobby of the May Dugan Center, 4115 Bridge Ave., to receive certificates for completion of their pre-clerical training. Keynote speaker was **Alice Butts**, wife of State Senator **Charles Butts**, and a trustee of Cuyahoga Community College.

The ceremony commended these students, most of whom are homemakers who have not been in a school setting for several years. Of the 16 who were graduated, three have already been hired into the clerical field and several others have signed on to attend classes at Tri-C to earn an associate degree.

The training program was developed in 1985 to offer entry-level training in math, English, typing and business skills at a neighborhood site.

JULIE'S JOTTINGS
JULIE SOWA

Artsy Clevelanders in 'landmark' event

The word has been spreading rapidly around the West Side. Now it is making forays into the east. What are we talking about? Why, word about the work of the Mae Dugan Westside Multi-Service Center, of course.

In 1988, the "People Helping People" campaign was established for the social services center on Bridge Avenue, with a goal of $2.8 million. These funds, to be raised in a variety of ways, are used for the programs most sought after by the neighborhood poor.

Last year's "Cleveland's Own" fund-raising event was held at the Beck Center in Lakewood and featured a variety of entertainment. Despite the fact that it was the first year for the benefit, it exceeded its goal both in terms of money raised and in the number of people who became aware of the center.

This year, "Cleveland's Own" will take place from 6:30-9 p.m. Nov. 18 in the Van Swerington Arcade at the Landmark Tower. It will feature displays of art by prominent NOVA artists and music from small groups stationed around the arcade. Select hors d'oeuvres and cocktails will be served all evening.

As usual, good-hearted suburbanites are the backbone of the endeavor to help the needy. Among those who are expected at "Cleveland's Own" are **Robert and Kathleen Pritchard, Thomas and Sandra Sullivan** and **Thomas and Elsa Pavlik** of Fairview Park; **Raymond Arth,** Mr. and Mrs. **Robert Mooney** and Mr. and Mrs. **James Mooney** of Westlake; Mr. and Mrs. **Thomas Code** of Bay Village and Mr. and Mrs. **William Grimberg** of Lakewood. **Holly Gigante,** also of Lakewood, is director of the center.

I'm sure the artistic talent of Cleveland will make just as big of an impression this year as the singing and dancing talent of Cleveland did last year. It should be a "landmark" event.

All cynicism aside, friends and neighbors of May Dugan West Side Service Center on Bridge Avenue are feeling thankful right now about outcome of their "Cleveland's Own" benefit reception held Saturday in the Van Sweringen Arcade. Around 225 people managed to fight the way through the aftermath of that nasty blizzard to help raise money center's worthwhile programs.

According to center spokeswoman **Patricia Ehlen,** $15,050 was the amount garnered as of Monday, and more donations are expected to a Ten pieces of artwork were sold out of the 30 displayed, all accomplish Cleveland artists. (Thus the name "Cleveland's Own.") Participants see the artwork and meet many of the artists, while munching on som cious food which went above and beyond the usual, humdrum hors d'oeuvres. Local musicians were also involved.

Adding to the festivities was the historical atmosphere of the recer renovated Landmark Office Towers, next to the Tower City Complex. ter of Ceremonies **Alan DePetro** of TV5, who has a personal interest things historic, explained that the arcade was once the old Midland B lobby.

Constructed in 1930 by the Van Sweringen brothers (who also buil Terminal Tower), its beauty was covered up in the '50s by a false ceilin other atrocities. Brought back to its former glory, the building is now to various shops and companies. If you are ever downtown, stop by th market Restaurant for a look-see. It is situated in the former bank's v and is a truly fascinating use of space.

Mary Caldwell, center board president, did a fine job of introduc Petro and recognizing Director **Holly Gigante** for her work at the cer Gigante's husband **Frank,** we hear, is getting real used to being greet with "Oh, so you're Holly Gigante's husband!" **Leslie Pritchard** and leen Pritchard were also honored for their fine work in co-chairing t benefit.

Fairview Park resident **Charles Tom** was the lucky winner of the ing. He will receive a package of gifts worth $1,500, including four din Johnny's Bar, tickets to the Cleveland Orchestra and men's and wom clothing.

Next month will bring to a close the 20th anniversary celebration center, which has been going on all year. Like DePetro said, thank go for places like the May Dugan Center which help people help themsel they have a chance to achieve happiness.

JULIE'S JOTTINGS
JULIE SOWA

THE PAST CAN SUPPORT THE FUTURE — Much enthusiasm is evident these days at the May Dugan West Side Multi-Service Center on Bridge Avenue. The cause for all the excitement is the Hometown Club, recently established by the center, said staffer **Patricia Ehlen.**

The idea for the club was formulated by "a group of Near West Side 'alumni' (former residents) who want to rekindle their enthusiasm in the area," said Ehlen. The group is referred to as the Hometown Club since it "consists of people who have an interest in the Near West Side because they lived in the area or had other roots in the area."

Club members come together to reminisce about the past and also support the future by helping out the various direct service programs offered at the center. They receive a mug, membership card, historical vignettes, a newsletter and the opportunity to volunteer at the center or donate books and food and participate in activities.

All this for a $20 membership donation each year.

Ehlen sent me one of the historical vignettes offered to members and it is a real gem for history buffs. It explains in a nutshell the development of the Near West Side, featuring names and locations.

The May Dugan center, incorporated in 1969, was named in tribute to a neighborhood woman who, in the 1930-40s, was a one-person counselor and advocate for her poor neighbors on the Near West Side. Programs at the independent, non-profit center are funded by foundations, public dollars and private citizens. Area residents govern the center.

To join the club, call 631-5800 or write Ehlen at the center, located at 4115 Bridge Ave., Cleveland 44113.

Cleveland has clams quivering with fright

If clams had legs, instead of just one foot, they would surely take off running whenever they heard our area being discussed. According to **Mary Conway Sullivan,** co-chair of the May Dugan West Side Multi-Service Center's "Sail-Abration," Cleveland is the clam bake capital of the world.

"In what Clevelanders call 'clam bake season,' September and October, more clams are brought into Cleveland than any other city in the country. In fact, Clevelanders buy so many clams in those two months that a strain is put on the market. In actuality, clams are in season all year round. No one seems to know exactly how or why Clevelanders got into this tradition of fall clam bakes, or why it caught on so successfully."

Sullivan should know whereof she speaks. She has recently married **T. Sean Sullivan,** owner of Navillus Gourmet Fish Co. which has recently relocated from Rocky River to 5221 Lorain Road, Cleveland. (Note that the company's name is the owner's name spelled backwards.)

The Sullivan family has long been involved in the worthy efforts of the May Dugan center, an independent neighborhood organization of the Near West Side of Cleveland governed by area residents and supported by people all over the west side. The center helps people by providing a wide range of social services such as housing, youth work, education and training, employment and family counseling. It is directed by **Holly Gigante** of Lakewood.

The Sail-Abration fund-raiser, set for 6 p.m. Saturday, Sept. 29, at the Nautica in the Flats, will be a clam and lobster bake including the usual seaside goodies: corn-on-the-cob, sweet potatoes, chicken and a light dessert. Sounds like no one will walk away hungry!

While the guests are digesting their food, they will be treated to the sounds of Impacto Nuevo, one of the hottest bands in the city. The Nautica Stage, itself, will be transformed to resemble a dock and Sullivan promises that the calypso and Caribbean tunes will "rock the dock." Other decorations will include large anchors on corporate tables designating those companies as "Anchors of the Community," the nautical colors of red, white and blue, and, for those purchasing the Admiral tickets, nifty white Admiral hats. Dress willl be nautical or casual.

Call **Patricia Ehlen,** May Dugan's resource developer, at 631-5800 to make your reservations.

Chapter 9
MANAGING OUR FINANCES

*F*rom the outset of the "People Helping People" campaign we felt it was essential that donors know that we were a reputable organization and that we handled our financial responsibilities properly. Our brochure states that our books are audited by a CPA and that funds raised are overseen by an Accounting Committee. We also filed for and received official verification of our campaign from the Greater Cleveland Growth Association (Chamber of Commerce), Charitable Solicitations Department in Columbus, and the Better Business Bureau.

We kept track of our income in a special ledger book. The book was divided into Program Pledges, Endowment Pledges, and separate pages for donations to each of the other Avenues. When a donation was received, it was first recorded in a receipt book. The bookkeeper also recorded the donor, date, amount, and balance due, if it was a pledge payment, on the appropriate ledger sheets. A copy of the receipt was given to the Resource Development Office. They recorded the payment in an alphabetically arranged binder which contained the name of the donor, kind of gift, the amount, and the date when a thank you note was sent. This dual system acted as an additional check.

As the campaign progressed and money began to come in, we had to be very accurate with our bookkeeping and follow General Accounting Procedures. Since many donations were given over a period of time, we kept track in the ledger and invoiced the donor for each payment. We also kept a control sheet for each ledger section which compiled monthly totals. Our financial advisors certainly encouraged unrestricted donations because it made bookkeeping simpler, but with a variety of fundraising methods, money was often contributed to a specific program. Our bookkeeping system managed to track all the various donations, but it was tedious.

Each entity we reported to, such as the Growth Association or the State of Ohio, required information in different categories. Since our books were set up to reflect our avenues, we had to leave paper trails for ourselves to be sure we matched the totals on all the reports.

During the campaign we received large amounts of money in one year. Because agencies like ours need to have an audit in order to get foundation money, we had to be certain to show accurately the money that came in for the campaign, but was not going to be used for that year. Our books needed to reflect income without appearing that we were earning more than we needed.

To deal with this problem, our financial advisors recommended that we categorize such funds as "Board Designated Funds", segregated from annual operating needs. These funds were made up of two accounts which our Board set up: 1) pledged funds whose use was restricted by the donors for programs, which we called "reserves", to be used when needed for those programs, and 2) an excess of income over expenses in a given year which we named the "May Dugan Fund" and earmarked strictly for new programs.

The Board Designated Funds are officially unrestricted program income and show as such on the audit sample below. They are tightly controlled and a two-thirds vote of the Board is necessary for their withdrawal. (See Figure 25)

During the final year of the Campaign, we began automating our books in an attempt to make the bookkeeping more efficient. If we had to do this over again, we'd computerize either before the Campaign or after it. Computerization is a project in itself!

Figure 25 STATEMENT OF REVENUE AND EXPENSES, MID-CAMPAIGN

THE NEAR WEST SIDE MULTI-SERVICE CORPORATION

STATEMENT OF SUPPORT, REVENUE AND EXPENSES

YEAR ENDED JANUARY 31,
(With Comparative Totals for the Year Ended January 31,

	Year Ended January 31,					Total All Funds	
	Unrestricted						
	Current Fund	(A) Board Designated Funds	Restricted Fund	Property Fund	Endowment Fund	Year Ended January 31, II	I
PUBLIC SUPPORT AND REVENUE:							
Public Support:							
Government grants	$	$	$ 216,103	$	$	$ 216,103	$ 184,290
Foundation grants		35,500	56,669			112,169	57,477
Corporate grants		32,950	18,664	20,000	37,000	88,614	35,881
Contributions - Other	9,120	46,760	25,323	22,397	27,700	131,300	89,230
Contributions - in-kind							3,050
Total public support	9,120	115,210	316,759	42,397	64,700	548,186	369,928
Revenue:							
Rental income	113,171					113,171	89,204
Investment income	17,481		365		1,434	19,280	8,755
Special events - net	15,086					15,086	16,495
Miscellaneous	12,341					12,341	11,184
Total revenue	158,079		365		1,434	159,878	125,638
Total public support and revenue	167,199	115,210	317,124	42,397	66,134	708,064	495,566
EXPENSES:							
Program services:							
Emergency assistance	9,598		87,437			97,035	96,288
Resource development	7,542		54,470			62,012	53,167
Employment/training	2,057		83,722			85,779	65,469
Neighborhood development	10,284		29,848			40,132	
Community outreach	3,771		30,731			34,502	52,543
Youth	1,028		16,118			17,146	15,284
Total program services	34,280		302,326			336,606	282,751
Supporting services:							
Management and general	34,667			1,343		36,010	29,507
Building operations	83,284			11,916		95,200	99,374
Total supporting services	117,951		-	13,259		131,210	128,881
Total expenses	152,231		302,326	13,259		467,816	411,632
EXCESS OF PUBLIC SUPPORT AND REVENUE OVER EXPENSES	$ 14,968	$ 115,210	$ 14,798	$ 29,138	$ 66,134	$ 240,248	$ 83,934

(A) Represents unrestricted contributions from the "People Helping People Campaign" which have been designated by the Board of Trustees as a designated fund for future operations and program development. Disbursements from this fund require the approval of a two-thirds majority of the Board of Trustees.

Chapter 10
THE FINE ART OF WRITING

*O*ur fund raising campaign was jam-packed with the written word. We wrote letters asking for money, follow-up letters, speeches, proposals, brochures, news releases, case statements and thank you notes, to name a few! There are many kinds of writing used in a major campaign like ours, the trick was to make that writing effective.

We have all received letters that just do not strike the right chord. Sometimes the writing seems confused, or too sappy, or even whiny. So, we reviewed our collective writing skills and developed techniques which enabled all of our writers to express themselves better.

The old reporter's adage of asking who, what, where, when, and why cannot be underestimated! These five questions forced the writer to analyze what he or she wanted to say, and to whom. Successful writing addressed the issues at hand, stated the particulars and concluded. It wasn't necessary to be dry, just short and to the point. Flowery prose is best left to Shakespeare; effective fund raisers are succinct.

Our General Appeal letters were an example of this kind of writing. We often wrote several versions of the same letter, depending upon the recipient. In all of them, we presented our case, listed ways for the recipient to help, noted the time frame of the appeal, and the monetary goal. We assumed that the reader knew nothing about us, and were as clear and straightforward as possible. The same approach applied to brochures, program descriptions, and news releases.

Writing thank you notes became easier with a simple "imaging" technique. We imagined that the person to whom the letter was being written was seated in front of us and we talked to this person. How would we say thank you? We wrote down what came to mind. This trick helped the writer focus on the individual and the note became more personal.

We attempted not to be "we" oriented in our writing. Inverting the sentence to emphasize the donor was a subtle, but significant, shift. "We need" became "You can help".

Good writing improved with practice. Reading what other agencies have written was also helpful, so we maintained a file of samples. These samples, though not perfect, illustrate the kind of writing that has worked for us. (See Figure 26)

Figure 26 WRITING SAMPLES

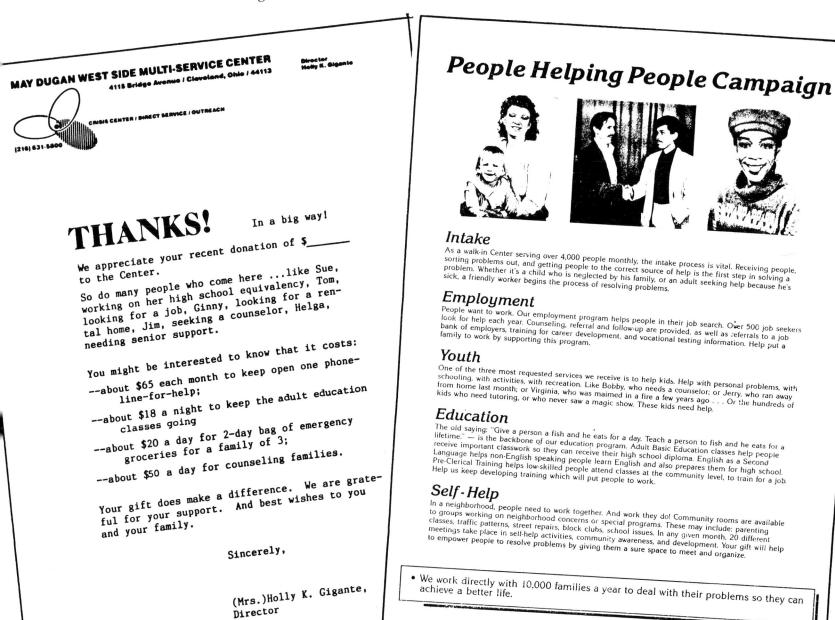

MAY DUGAN WEST SIDE MULTI-SERVICE CENTER
4115 Bridge Avenue / Cleveland, Ohio / 44113

Director
Holly K. Gigante

CRISIS CENTER / DIRECT SERVICE / OUTREACH

(216) 631-5800

THANKS!

In a big way!

We appreciate your recent donation of $_____ to the Center.

So do many people who come here ...like Sue, working on her high school equivalency, Tom, looking for a job, Ginny, looking for a rental home, Jim, seeking a counselor, Helga, needing senior support.

You might be interested to know that it costs:

--about $65 each month to keep open one phone-line-for-help;

--about $18 a night to keep the adult education classes going

--about $20 a day for 2-day bag of emergency groceries for a family of 3;

--about $50 a day for counseling families.

Your gift does make a difference. We are grateful for your support. And best wishes to you and your family.

Sincerely,

(Mrs.)Holly K. Gigante,
Director

People Helping People Campaign

Intake

As a walk-in Center serving over 4,000 people monthly, the intake process is vital. Receiving people, sorting problems out, and getting people to the correct source of help is the first step in solving a problem. Whether it's a child who is neglected by his family, or an adult seeking help because he's sick, a friendly worker begins the process of resolving problems.

Employment

People want to work. Our employment program helps people in their job search. Over 500 job seekers look for help each year. Counseling, referral and follow-up are provided, as well as referrals to a job bank of employers, training for career development, and vocational testing information. Help put a family to work by supporting this program.

Youth

One of the three most requested services we receive is to help kids. Help with personal problems, with schooling, with activities, with recreation. Like Bobby, who needs a counselor; or Jerry, who ran away from home last month; or Virginia, who was maimed in a fire a few years ago . . . Or the hundreds of kids who need tutoring, or who never saw a magic show. These kids need help.

Education

The old saying: "Give a person a fish and he eats for a day. Teach a person to fish and he eats for a lifetime." — is the backbone of our education program. Adult Basic Education classes help people receive important classwork so they can receive their high school diploma. English as a Second Language helps non-English speaking people learn English and also prepares them for high school. Pre-Clerical Training helps low-skilled people attend classes at the community level, to train for a job. Help us keep developing training which will put people to work.

Self-Help

In a neighborhood, people need to work together. And work they do! Community rooms are available to groups working on neighborhood concerns or special programs. These may include: parenting classes, traffic patterns, street repairs, block clubs, school issues. In any given month, 20 different meetings take place in self-help activities, community awareness, and development. Your gift will help to empower people to resolve problems by giving them a sure space to meet and organize.

- We work directly with 10,000 families a year to deal with their problems so they can achieve a better life.

Sample "thank you" letters

Page from Campaign brochure

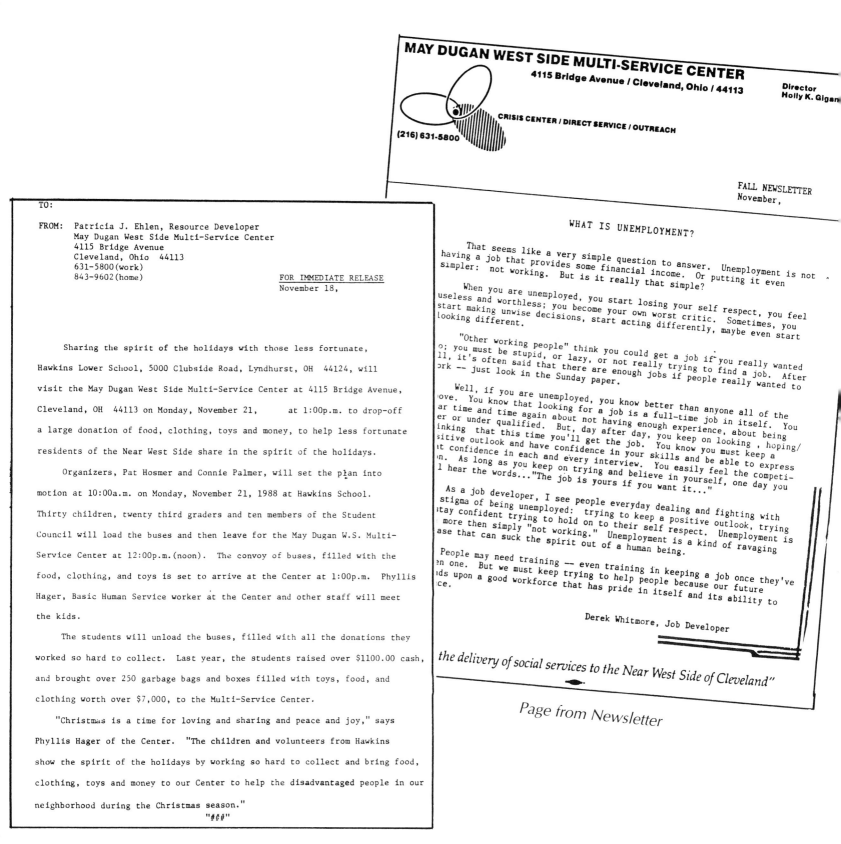

MAY DUGAN WEST SIDE MULTI-SERVICE CENTER
4115 Bridge Avenue / Cleveland, Ohio / 44113

Director
Holly K. Gigan

CRISIS CENTER / DIRECT SERVICE / OUTREACH

(216) 631-5800

FALL NEWSLETTER
November,

WHAT IS UNEMPLOYMENT?

That seems like a very simple question to answer. Unemployment is not having a job that provides some financial income. Or putting it even simpler: not working. But is it really that simple?

When you are unemployed, you start losing your self respect, you feel useless and worthless; you become your own worst critic. Sometimes, you start making unwise decisions, start acting differently, maybe even start looking different.

"Other working people" think you could get a job if you really wanted to; you must be stupid, or lazy, or not really trying to find a job. After all, it's often said that there are enough jobs if people really wanted to work -- just look in the Sunday paper.

Well, if you are unemployed, you know better than anyone all of the above. You know that looking for a job is a full-time job in itself. You hear time and time again about not having enough experience, about being over or under qualified. But, day after day, you keep on looking , hoping/thinking that this time you'll get the job. You know you must keep a positive outlook and have confidence in your skills and be able to express that confidence in each and every interview. You easily feel the competition. As long as you keep on trying and believe in yourself, one day you'll hear the words..."The job is yours if you want it..."

As a job developer, I see people everyday dealing and fighting with stigma of being unemployed: trying to keep a positive outlook, trying stay confident trying to hold on to their self respect. Unemployment is more then simply "not working." Unemployment is a kind of ravaging ease that can suck the spirit out of a human being.

People may need training — even training in keeping a job once they've en one. But we must keep trying to help people because our future ds upon a good workforce that has pride in itself and its ability to ce.

Derek Whitmore, Job Developer

the delivery of social services to the Near West Side of Cleveland"

Page from Newsletter

TO:

FROM: Patricia J. Ehlen, Resource Developer
May Dugan West Side Multi-Service Center
4115 Bridge Avenue
Cleveland, Ohio 44113
631-5800(work)
843-9602(home)

FOR IMMEDIATE RELEASE
November 18,

Sharing the spirit of the holidays with those less fortunate, Hawkins Lower School, 5000 Clubside Road, Lyndhurst, OH 44124, will visit the May Dugan West Side Multi-Service Center at 4115 Bridge Avenue, Cleveland, OH 44113 on Monday, November 21, at 1:00p.m. to drop-off a large donation of food, clothing, toys and money, to help less fortunate residents of the Near West Side share in the spirit of the holidays.

Organizers, Pat Hosmer and Connie Palmer, will set the plan into motion at 10:00a.m. on Monday, November 21, 1988 at Hawkins School. Thirty children, twenty third graders and ten members of the Student Council will load the buses and then leave for the May Dugan W.S. Multi-Service Center at 12:00p.m.(noon). The convoy of buses, filled with the food, clothing, and toys is set to arrive at the Center at 1:00p.m. Phyllis Hager, Basic Human Service worker at the Center and other staff will meet the kids.

The students will unload the buses, filled with all the donations they worked so hard to collect. Last year, the students raised over $1100.00 cash, and brought over 250 garbage bags and boxes filled with toys, food, and clothing worth over $7,000, to the Multi-Service Center.

"Christmas is a time for loving and sharing and peace and joy," says Phyllis Hager of the Center. "The children and volunteers from Hawkins show the spirit of the holidays by working so hard to collect and bring food, clothing, toys and money to our Center to help the disadvantaged people in our neighborhood during the Christmas season."

"#⍧#"

Press Release

We can't leave this chapter without talking about proposals. If you thought this book would save you from ever having to write another proposal, then you may be disappointed.

All the money we raised came from some kind of writing or another. Even with all the wonderful new supporters and new ways of raising money we still had the grueling task of writing hundreds of proposals. Some were two pages, others thirty , but they all took some time to prepare. We followed the guidelines of each foundation and they were all different. We wrote some proposals two and three times over and we even developed a "master" format for a proposal which we hoped we could modify for each foundation. The master proposal worked in some cases but it didn't work for many others. Personal contact was helpful because many proposals we sent "cold" didn't get us anywhere. Nevertheless, we did a lot of proposal writing and learned as we went along.

Chapter 11
WHEN OPPOR-TUNITY KNOCKS

*W*e learned that the "social worker mentality" is a liability in a resource development campaign. A "resource awareness mentality" is the other side of that coin. Throughout our campaign, we looked for situations or circumstances which could be used to our advantage, creatively incorporating everything from national holidays to obscure traditions into our fund raising program.

The Center's 20th Anniversary, for example, happened to fall during the "People Helping People" campaign. This was a great opportunity! Our planning included a variety of anniversary related activities. We celebrated with t-shirts, a yard party, a Community Awards Luncheon, and other events. We rubber stamped "Our 20th Year" on everything. In doing so, we generated community awareness of the Center, and as a by-product, stimulated donations into our development campaign. (See Figure 27)

Figure 27 20TH ANNIVERSARY PLANS.

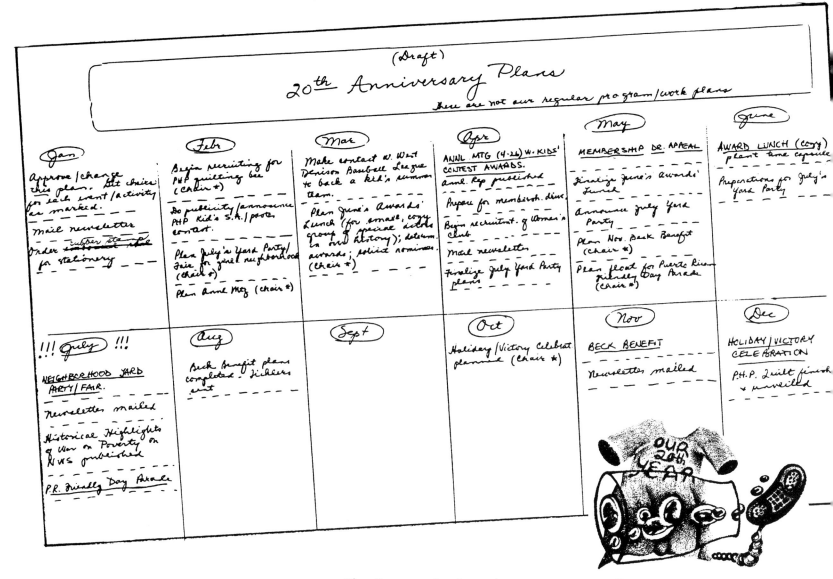

The Community Awards were an especially good idea. We took a great deal of time to decide what kinds of awards we wanted to give and to whom they should be presented. We chose five different awards and recipients varied from a local postman to our congressperson. We presented the "Awards of Appreciation" at a luncheon and invited Board and Committee members, staff, volunteers, and friends. Ideally these awards

will be presented on a biennial basis without the anniversary "hook".
(See Figure 28)

Figure 28 AWARDS OF APPRECIATION

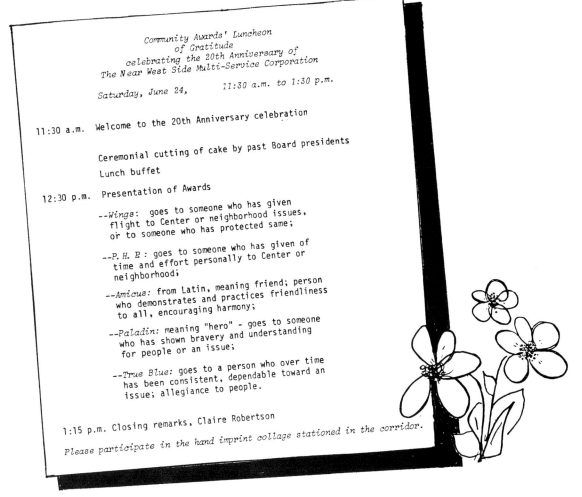

Community Awards' Luncheon
of Gratitude
celebrating the 20th Anniversary of
The Near West Side Multi-Service Corporation

Saturday, June 24,   11:30 a.m. to 1:30 p.m.

11:30 a.m. Welcome to the 20th Anniversary celebration

Ceremonial cutting of cake by past Board presidents

Lunch buffet

12:30 p.m. Presentation of Awards

--*Wings*: goes to someone who has given
flight to Center or neighborhood issues,
or to someone who has protected same;

--*P. H. B*: goes to someone who has given of
time and effort personally to Center or
neighborhood;

--*Amicus*: from Latin, meaning friend; person
who demonstrates and practices friendliness
to all, encouraging harmony;

--*Paladin*: meaning "hero" - goes to someone
who has shown bravery and understanding
for people or an issue;

--*True Blue*: goes to a person who over time
has been consistent, dependable toward an
issue; allegiance to people.

1:15 p.m. Closing remarks, Claire Robertson

Please participate in the hand imprint collage stationed in the corridor.

The Neighborhood Development Demonstration Project (NDDP) provided another opportunity. We received this grant from the government to expand our Evening Hours Program. The NDDP stipulated that if we could raise $7,500 in our immediate neighborhood the federal government would match it 4 to 1 for a total of $37,500. We had never focused on raising money this way. The opportunity to raise this kind of money in our neighborhood stimulated a variety of activities, and motivated neighborhood people to believe in their ability to make a difference.

We went door-to-door on a Sunday afternoon and raised over $700 ! We had a phone-a-thon. We put a large water jug in the lobby and collected loose change. We had a Yard Party, bake sales, t-shirt sales and car washes — all in our immediate area. The NDDP also served as an impetus to develop local awareness of the Center, increase donations, and develop new fundraising methods. The NDDP gave us the idea to try going after more matching grants. For example, we asked one foundation to give us a two to one match for our Emergency Food Program; for every dollar we raised in the neighborhood we asked them to give us two.

Sometimes, circumstances worked to our advantage. The first "Cleveland's Own" benefit, for example, came together like puzzle pieces. The location was available and reasonably priced, one of our Board members had artistic acquaintances, someone else knew a caterer. We were aware of these factors and put them together to create our first major event, a variety show/cocktail party.

We have capitalized on Mother's Day, using it as an opportunity to sell cards through our Business Endeavors avenue. We have taken obscure occasions like St. Nicholas Day and used it to stimulate donations. (See Figure 29)

Figure 29 ST. NICHOLAS DAY GREETING

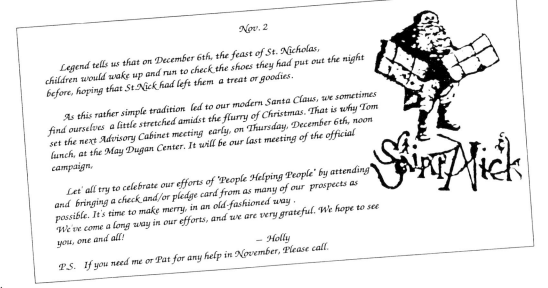

Nov. 2

Legend tells us that on December 6th, the feast of St. Nicholas, children would wake up and run to check the shoes they had put out the night before, hoping that St. Nick had left them a treat or goodies.

As this rather simple tradition led to our modern Santa Claus, we sometimes find ourselves a little stretched amidst the flurry of Christmas. That is why Tom set the next Advisory Cabinet meeting early, on Thursday, December 6th, noon lunch, at the May Dugan Center. It will be our last meeting of the official campaign,

Let' all try to celebrate our efforts of 'People Helping People' by attending and bringing a check and/or pledge card from as many of our prospects as possible. It's time to make merry, in an old-fashioned way. We've come a long way in our efforts, and we are very grateful. We hope to see you, one and all!

— Holly

P.S. If you need me or Pat for any help in November, Please call.

Christmas in July, spring white sales, the possibilities are endless. Creativity is an essential part of fund raising. Looking at life with a perceptive eye and applying that to the agency's situation is the "resource awareness mentality."

"Helpers of all ages!"

Celebrating many helping hands of 20 years,

Local church recognized for helping the homeless in our neighborhood.

Community Awards' recipients.

Development staff hard at work.

Chapter 12
EXPRESSING OUR APPRECIATION

*T*o say "thank you" for a gift is simply good manners. In the case of fund raising, saying "thank you" is absolutely vital. People like to be appreciated! As organizations develop relationships with donors, they must perpetually show their appreciation, and there is a diversity of ways to show gratitude.

It is important to keep good records of what has been given and how it has been acknowledged. While this may require internal planning and some expenditure, we found that the time and money invested in saying "thank you" for a gift is well spent. Forgetting a gift could jeopardize a carefully cultivated relationship.

Appreciation does not have to be public. Many donors avoid the limelight, preferring a private expression of gratitude. Sometimes a sincere "thank you" note or personal conversation is more than enough. Others might need a more visible acknowledgment.

Every donor is special and unique. The expression of gratitude to that donor should also be special and unique. This can only be accomplished by taking the time to get to know donors and responding to them personally.

Some fund raising books indicate a ratio between the amount of the gift and the gesture of appreciation. A large donation, might have a corresponding building or room named for the donor.

Sometimes a job becomes a form of appreciation and gives volunteers the feeling of being "insiders". For example, one of our loyal volunteers was asked to write Christmas cards to about 150 close friends of the Center, and include a brief personal message on each. The volunteer knew that we respected her talents and abilities.

A couple who are members of the Advisory Board treated some prospective donors to a tour of the Center and dinner at a local restaurant. Their graciousness made them effective fund raisers, and they knew how important their efforts were to the Center.

A neighborhood woman spent many hours attending Center luncheons, meeting prospective donors, and telling them about the neighborhood. Her role as a local resident, not a paid staff member, created a bond between the prospects and the neighborhood. She was an inspiration to many donors and an invaluable asset to the Center. And, she knew how important her help was.

A donor who receives a personal, handwritten note feels like more than a "checkbook". Even a form letter on which a personalized note has been scrawled conveys the sense of belonging. First time donors who receive notes which welcome them into the Center's work and express the desire to get better acquainted, feel important. Notes need not be long, or written on expensive stationery or in flowery verse, but they must be written from the heart.

We found that often it was easier to write personal notes than form letters, especially to our inner core of donors. For example, a note which reads, "Susan, thanks so much for all your work last week. You really made things run smoothly. You're the best!", conveyed sincere appreciation. Of course, such notes are easier to write if one truly knows the recipient. We used cards in a variety of sizes and shapes, clip-art symbols, stickers, etc. We wanted to have responses that showed special thought. Sometimes a blank sheet of paper with a gold star on it, or a copy of a cartoon or poem on a special interest was sent. Other methods of saying thanks were a quick phone call, a birthday card, a mention in a newsletter, a lunch, or a "Certificate of Appreciation".

Sometimes creative ways to show appreciation presented themselves. For example, after discussing a certain topic with a volunteer, a magazine article on the subject was located, xeroxed and mailed to that person with appropriate comments in the margin. A volunteer couple who not only made a large financial gift, but were tireless workers on the campaign were thanked with one pink rose and a sincere note. We knew that no conventional thank you could be adequate, it had to be symbolic.

We have also found that asking for advice on a subject from a knowledgeable supporter, having coffee together, discussing a report, sharing good news and even a wink or a hug, are welcomed. Dedicating a newsletter or an annual report to someone are also possibilities. Even discussion or bantering over an issue can show appreciation and respect.

We have worked diligently to design awards which are creative and recognize special donors of our campaign, (See Figure30, page 110).

PLATINUM PROFILE AWARD	- Gifts of $200,000 and over
GOLDEN KEY AWARD	- Gifts of $100,000 and over
SILVER STAR AWARD	- Gifts of $50,000 and over
BRONZE MEDALLION AWARD	- Gifts of $25,000 and over
BRASS MEDALLION AWARD	- Gifts of $10,000 and over
COPPER MEDALLION AWARD	- Gifts of $5,000 and over

Figure 30 SPECIAL DONOR AWARDS

Volunteers and donors are the backbone of a fund raising campaign. Sincere appreciation of their work is vital to campaign success. We are all donors and we are all receivers at different times. Appreciation pulls donors and receivers together in a common "human" denominator and is felt at a much deeper level when we recognize how many people can be served by our efforts. That really is at the heart of volunteering.

Former Board President, Connie Smiddie, presents a Community Award.

Volunteer and staff work together.

Board and Staff greet friends and neighbors.

George Keith, campaign advisor, and Holly K.Gigante, Director, enjoy victory celebration.

Board Members Nancy, Pat, and V.A. talk over fundraising plans.

Chapter 13
WHAT EXPERIENCE HAS TAUGHT US

*W*hen we began our three-year fund raising program, we were rookies, both volunteers and staff. This experience, however, has taught us about the art of resource development. As a result, this is what we would do the next time:

- Involve everyone connected with the agency in the fund raising effort.
- Be in it with "two feet" from the start; fundraising is hard work.
- Have all leadership people make a financial donation.
- Include people with a variety of contacts on Advisory Cabinet.
- Be true to the character/charisma of the agency.

113

- Aim high in setting goals.
- Try to have several "heavy hitters" on your Cabinet.
- Establish office systems at the start of the campaign and stick with the systems chosen.
- Develop a large mailing list and work at keeping it current.
- Set a time line for the campaign and evaluate progress along the way.
- Spend time planning.
- Consider a variety of fund raising techniques then READ, READ, READ about each.
- Choose methods which are suited to the agency, the workers, and the time frame.
- Try not to choose more methods than can be realistically handled.
- Offer a variety of ways to make donations.
- Be creative.
- "Do the arithmetic first," in preparing for any Event.
- Make certain that Events will make money and be fun
- Go out and get donors; they won't automatically come to you.
- Be able to take rejection.
- Remember that donors are people first.
- Aim to be classy, not extravagant.
- Make volunteers feel as important as they are.
- Give volunteers jobs which suit them.
- Have a "TO DO" list of activities and a "NEEDS" list available for volunteers/prospective donors.
- Invite people to visit the agency; tours produce both volunteers and donors.
- Ask for money! Rich usually ask rich. Poor usually ask poor.
- Use both intelligence and intuition in asking for money.
- Have all requests for money and in-kind support originate from one office.
- Send solicitors in pairs when going door-to-door, It is easier and more fun.
- Work on developing a "grapevine".

- Work for as much media coverage as possible.
- Cultivate the media over time.
- Keep meticulous financial records.
- Read the literature of other agencies, and keep interesting copies for reference.
- Keep samples of your own literature.
- Learn how to write many proposals.
- Do as much camera-ready printing as possible.
- Use clip art when effective.
- Proofread everything!
- Have a concise case statement for your needs.
- Speak from the heart in all communications.
- Be concise.
- Don't take anything for granted.
- Listen to your donors.
- Be open to suggestions or ideas which might further the campaign.
- Always have agendas with purpose and action for meetings.
- Thank everyone for their gift of money, time, or services.
- Find creative ways to say "Thank You".
- Devise unique gift recognition methods

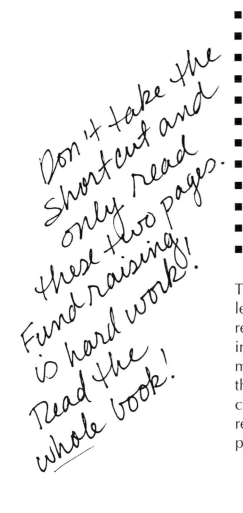

Don't take the shortcut and only read these two pages. Fund raising is hard work! Read the whole book!

This experience taught us a great deal about fund raising, but the best lesson that we learned is that people WANT to help other people, — real people, not vague, bureaucratic agencies. The communications and interaction among people of all backgrounds was as important as the money we raised. They developed continuing personal relationships as they worked to achieve a common goal. The "People Helping People" campaign built a financial foundation for the May Dugan Center as it reinforced the human framework that has always been the Center's purpose. We continue to build upon that foundation.

BIBLIOGRAPHY

— some books and resources we found helpful

Ashton, Debra. THE COMPLETE GUIDE TO PLANNED GIVING. Cambridge, Mass: JLA Publications, XXXX

Brentlinger, Marilyn E. THE ULTIMATE BENEFIT BOOK: How to Raise $50,000 Plus for your organization. Cleveland, Ohio: Octavia Press, 1987.

Broce, Thomas E. FUNDRAISING: THE GUIDE TO RAISING MONEY FROM PRIVATE SOURCES. Norman: University of Oklahoma Press, 1986.

Conrad, Daniel Lunn. TECHNIQUES OF FUND-RAISING. Secaucus, N.J.: L. Stuart, 1974.

Drothing, Phillip T. PUTTING THE FUN IN FUND RAISING. Chicago: Contemporary Books, 1979.

Dunn, Thomas G. HOW TO SHAKE THE NEW MONEY TREE: Creative Fund Raising for Today's Nonprofit Organizations. New York: Penguin Books, 1988.

Flanagan, Joan. THE GRASSROOTS FUND RAISING BOOK: How to Raise Money in Your Community. Chicago: Swallow Press, 1977.

Lant, Jeffery. DEVELOPMENT TODAY: A Fund Raising Guide for Nonprofit Organizations. Cambridge, Mass.: JLA Publications, 1990

Lant, Jeffrey. MONEY MAKING MARKETING: Find the People Who Need What You're Selling and Making Sure They Buy It. Cambridge, Mass.: JLA Publications, 1987.

Lefferts, Robert. GETTING A GRANT: How to Write Successful Grant Proposals. Englewood Cliffs, N.J.: Prentice Hall, 1978.

Mirkin, Howard R. THE COMPLETE FUND RAISING GUIDE. New York: Public Service Materials Center, 1988.

THE NONPROFIT ENTREPRENEUR: Creating Ventures to Earn Income. New York, N.Y.: Foundation Center, 1988.

THE ONE, TWO, THREE OF DEVELOPING A MARKETING PLAN: Marketing Strategy for the Nonprofit Organization. Cleveland, Ohio: Discover Marketing Innovations, 1990.

Schneiter, Paul H. and Nelson, Donald T. THE 13 MOST COMMON FUNDRAISING MISTAKES - AND HOW TO AVOID THEM. Washington, D.C.: Taft Corp.

Seymour, Harold. DESIGNS FOR FUNDRAISING.

Taylor, Bernard P.GUIDE TO SUCCESSFUL FUND RAISING FOR AUTHENTIC CHARITABLE PURPOSES. South Plainfield, N.J.: Groupwork Today, 1976

Warner, Irving R. THE ART OF FUND RAISING. New York: Harper & Row, 1975

Weinberger, Jane D. PLEASE BUY MY VIOLETS, or How To Raise Money For Your Causes. Mr. Desert, Me.: WindSwept House,1986.

Young, Joyce. FUNDRAISING FOR NON-PROFIT GROUPS: How to Get Money From Corporations. Seattle, Washington: International Self-Counsel Press,1981.

Chapter 14
EPILOGUE

On May 10,1991 a celebration was held, marking the conclusion of the "People Helping People" Campaign. Thirty-two donors, who made contributions of $5,000 or more, were presented with lucite awards embedded with metal medallions. Many photographs were taken and recognition was made of the remarkable accomplishments of the campaign.

When the "party was over", however, we realized that coming down from a successful campaign and continuing to collect annual funds is extremely difficult. Even though we raised $1.2 million, and volunteers, donors and staff members were tired, annual bills still require payment, obligations still have to be met. There is little time to savor the success. While it is natural to experience a letdown, we need to remind ourselves that fund raising is a constant. We must begin again.

After all the work of the campaign, we could not let the contacts and resources we developed evaporate, even though the pledges were paid. We had to follow-up and stay in touch with past donors and make new ones.

Proposals, even for small items, require accurate preparation and careful writing; we already knew that. But the lesson of the campaign was that we must also make phone calls, write letters and maintain contacts if we were to have our proposals granted. Expecting even previous donors to give again without the set-up and preparation done during the campaign is unrealistic.

One of our donors told us that he originally became involved with the Center for three reasons. First he admired our "passion and persistence". Second, he was impressed that another company had demonstrated confidence in us by giving us some stock. Third, he noted that local small businesses were involved with the Center. Not losing sight of the qualities which bought donors into the Center, and continuing to develop and enthusiastically expand on those qualities is a tall order, but essential to ongoing fund raising activities.

Our fourth annual benefit might have fallen victim to the post-campaign letdown if we had permitted it. We couldn't find an eager chairperson to undertake the event, and even considered skipping it. But previous events had generated $15,000 to $25,000, too much money to give up on so easily. So the decision was made to proceed with the benefit, but to simplify it. The director of the Center, a Board member, one steadfast volunteer and the staff organized the event, choosing a country-western theme, locating a band, a caterer and a site.

Once the word was out that the benefit was on, volunteers caught the spirit. We're "back-in-the-saddle again" with several committees involved and the preparation is moving along very well. The point is, we just cannot give up! The Director must show the leadership necessary to keep the fund-raising effort alive and well.

With the close of the campaign, the Advisory Cabinet was officially dissolved. However, we wanted to somehow retain the members and augment our Board. Many Cabinet members were important in the success of the campaign, and we value their contributions. We have then, established an Advisory Committee to the Board of Directors made up of some former Advisory Cabinet members, as well as others who are interested in our work. This group will meet only twice a year and will act to raise funds for the Center.

Other changes have been experienced since the close of the campaign. The Resource Development staff is now faced with some major adjustments. How will we continue to raise money? Which avenues should we pursue? Which should we delete? Should we have the Ladies Teas? the Business Luncheons? the Hometown Club? What other sources of revenues can we investigate? The pace of activity has changed somewhat. New goals have been set, new plans made. Leadership is still vital, from the Director, the Board and the staff, to keep our Resource Development activities in gear.

Looking back, we see that what was important during the campaign continues to be important: leadership, personal contact with donors and volunteers, appreciation for work done. These are all basic within the structure of the campaign, and outside it!

The fanfare, the excitement and the hoopla of the campaign may end, but the commitment to fund raising never does!

Colophon

This book was designed and illustrated by the students of the
Community Graphics class at The Cleveland Institute of Art.
        Design: Mahlia Mahan
                Margaret Smith
    Illustration: Tony Lutzo
                D'Wayne Murphy
                Jan Tumilowicz
                Katherine Mason
      Production
            and
cover design: Margaret Smith

The text is set in Adobe Optima, the chapter headings
in Adobe New Century Schoolbook, the initials are Adobe
Freestyle Script.

This book was produced and funded by a grant
from The Cleveland Foundation and printed
by The Orange Blossom Press at Cleveland, Ohio
in the year 1991.

Volunteers on our Resource Development Project

AARP Helpers
Christine Adkins
Josie Ahmad
Tom Alemagno
Pauline Allen

Judith Allen
Richard Anderson
Florine Armbruster
Joel & Jose Arroyo
Irma Arroyo

Ebony B.
Brenda Bacety
Cynthia Bailey
Dede Baker
Mary Baronak

Tom Bartell
Mary Bass
Brian Beargie
Arturo Becerra
Larry Belt

June Benson
Anita Berk
Regina Bing
Jolie Bishop
Angel Black

Juanita Blackshere
Steve Bodnar
Brad Bond
Jenny Borven
Mary Borzi

Shama Brahms
Kathy Brandi
Goldie Bratsch
Molly & Dan Brenghouse
Bob Brent

Claudia Brittenham
Bertie Brooks
Ron Brown
Becky Bruno
Terry Burgess

Christine Burton
Alice Butts
Esteban Cabezas
Bobbie Caldwell
Mary Caldwell

William Caldwell
Wilma Cales
Mimi Camacho

Grace Campbell
Edward Carlson

Jeannette Carlson
Christine Carreon
Jean Castelle
Benita Chesholm
Roy Chiles

Jim Chura
Barbara Code
Cindy Code
Bonita Colbert
Lalita Cole

Linda Cole
Della Colegrove
Mary Colegrove
Marilyn Conti
Maridell Conture

Debbie Conway
Yolanda Cooper
Judy Corrigan
Jane Cosby
Michelle/Regina Cosme

Terri Cottos
James Craciun
Jim Crisp
Karen Cupp
Christine Cyr

Betty Daniels
Marilyn Dant
Hubert Darling
Billy Daugherty
Jack Daugherty

Betty Davies
Janet Davis
Juanita Davis
Nikki Davis
Tenisha Davis

Norma Deavers
Helen DiBin
Chris Dickey
Leroy Dickey
Nikki Dillon

Debbie Dinner
Christine Dorko
Stephanie Dorko
Laura Dumchus
Judy Dunn

Irene Ebush
Larry "Jack" Eck
Dick Ehlen
Maryann Ehlen
Patricia Ehlen

Mary Ellen Eickman-Fiala
Michelle Elsworth
Mary Englert
Sharon Erick
Mark Erml

Edith Espinosa
Bob Estep
Carol Estep
Charles Estep
Dale Estep

Robert Estep
Rodney Estep
Ruth Estep
Betty Fancher
Colleen Feighan

Pat Feighan
Alfredo R. Feliciano
Jose Feliciano
Ted Feliciano
Ursula Fernandez

Arguello Figueroa
Glenna Fischer
Robert Fischer
Dale Fisher
Denise Fitzwater

Mary Flanagan
Darlene Fleming
Kristie Fleming
Sheila Fleming
Vanessa Fleming

Richard Foster
Melissa Fox
Olga Fricke
Michael Friedman
Misty Friend

Carol Froelick
Peggy Fugate
Cheryl Gayhart
Sandi Gerena
Jennifer Gerenscer

Frank Gigante
Holly K. Gigante
Maria Gigante
Nick Gigante
Peggy Gilkerson

Peggy Gillard
Louis Gillich
Kitty Gillund
Tom Ginter
Andrei Gnepp

Marcus Gonzalez
Joel Gorski
Bridget Grady

Ellen Grady
Kathy Grady

Pat Grady
Marge Granzier
Lee Griffin
Brian Grimberg
Kate Grimberg

Susan Grimberg
William Grimberg
Hazel Grizzell
Richard Gudat
Michael Gunter

Maria Guzman
Jean Haas
Jeanette Hager
Phyllis Hager
Joe Haggerty

Katherine Hahnel
Susan Halle
Ann Hannah
Anna Hark
Lanese Harris

Debra Haviland
Charles Heidel
Karen Heller
Maryanne Henderson
Betty & Joan Hendricks

Mary Hendricks
Lillian Hengoed
Ted Henry
Tricia Heraghty
Chris Holmes

Jennifer Holmes
Shelby Holmes de Reyes
Audrey Holt
Sherri Holt
Lee Ann Honda

Charlene Horton
Dick Horton
Chuck Hoven
Madelyne Huber
Chris/Joe/Mike Huges

Paul Hurst
Tim Hyland
Andrea Jackson
Dave Jacobs
Vi James

Bill Jenks
Charlotte Jennings
Donald Jennings
Ethel Jennings
Michael Jennings

Deborah Johns
Ricky Johnston
Sherman Johnston
Brenda Jones
John Jones

Ali Kapelow
George M. Keith
Marietta Kelly
Mike Ketterick
Debbie Kilbane

Ed Kilbane, Jr.
Ed and V.A. Kilbane
Katie Kilbane
Patrick Kilbane
Cathy Kilner

Jenny Kim
Andrea King
Bonita King
Jon King
Carol Kirk

Tenisha Kitchen
Angela Kitiso
Kesty Kizevicus
Terry Klima
Cheri Knight

Malvina Kollar
Paul Kollar
Christie Kovack
Ann Krueger
Bobby Krueger

Danny Krueger
Don Kuehn
Jayne Kuhnen
Jason Kuhlman
Geoff Kukla

Mary Lafferty
Lillian LaBoy
Pat LaFlamme
Joe La Guardia
Josephine LaMattino

Estelle Lamiell
John Lane
Pat Lawless
Nancy Lee
Robert Lee

Bracy Lewis
Rachel Likes
Francis Linton
Dorothy LoGalbo
Gina LoGalbo

John LoGalbo
Jack Lombardo
Betty Long

Gina Lucarelli
Enrique Lunarie

Tony Lutzo
Jeff Mackert
James Malik
April Malloy
Jack Malone

Jason Maloof
Mike Maloof
Melinda Mangan
David Maraldo
Jeff Marks

Walter Martens
Carol Matty
Frank Matty
Ed Matuszewski
Matt Mazany

Maggie McCormick
Maggie McIntyre
Mary Kay McManamon
Kevin McLaughlin
Judy McLaughlin

Doris McLoughlin
John McLoughlin
James Mesker
Sonia Meyers
Jennifer Miecznikowski

Loreen Miecznikowski
Pat Mielnik
Jerry Mieyal
Eleonor Mihiel
Charles Miller

Reni Miller
Matthew Mohawk
Chuck Molcsany
Paulina Molina
Therese Moltz

Janet Mooney
Maggie Mooney
Betty Moore
Carla Murico
Sharon Murphy

Jason Murton
Linda Murton
JoAnn Nagy
Ray Niewirdomski
Charlene Nicholson

Jacquelyn Niesen
Robert Norlin
Marge Norton
Richard Nosse
Randy Nottingham

Lawrence Oakar
Mary Rose Oakar
Roberto Ocasio
Elaine O'Grodnik
Nancy Ohliger

Betty Ortiz
Santos Ortiz
Thomas Park
Nicole Parobek
Vickie Parobek

Marie Patterson
Jeanette Patton
Maxine Patton
Tamera Patton
Winona Paul

Hugh Pavlovich
John Perera
Connie Perry
Robin Peterson
Mary Petitt

Stephanie Pettis
Doris & Greg Pilgrim
William Plato
Meghan Platten
Rhonda Pridemore

Beth Pritchard
Dale Pritchard
Kathleen Pritchard
Leslie Pritchard
Robert D. Pritchard

Reid Proctor
Erma Pugh
Angela Quinones
Belinda Quinones
John Raffo

Josie Ramirez
Jose Ramos
John Ranally
Karen Ratliff
Beth Raymond

Christine Reel
Donald Reel, Jr.
Donald Reel, Sr.
Cathy Reeves
Karen Rego

Anne Reitter
Dani Ripich
Terry Ripich
Cindy Rivera
Evelyn Rivera

Claire Robertson
Debbie & Denver Robertson
Diana Robertson

Heather Robertson
James Robertson

Latyna Robertson
Sean Robertson
Seantele Robertson
Wayne Robertson
Larry Rock

Arlene Rodriguez
David Rodriguez
Jose L. Rodriguez, Jr.
Ronald Rogers
Karen Roggenburk

Carol Romano
Kelly Romano
Phillip Romano
Angelo Rosario
Maureen Rothmann

Alvin Ruiz
James A. Rusnov
Leslie Sabbagh
Carol Sabo
Dave Sacco

Dolores Sacco
Carol Sanders
Debbie Sanders
James Sanders
James Sanders, Jr.

Charles Scavelli
Gerhardt Schmidt
Jean Schriner
John Schriner
Katie Schriner

Russ Schroeder
Robert & Libby Schultz
Dan Schwarzer
Willie Senquiz
Dawn Sharrer

Doug Sharrer
John Sharrer
Junior Sharrer
Leona Sharrer
Pat Sharrer

Scott Sharrer
John Shimko
Robert Shores
Matt Simmons
Ann Slack

Ed Slack
Jessica Slivka
Michael Slivka
Ngan & Charles Slivka
Matt & Sandy Slocum

Connie Smiddie
Charmaine Smith
Linda Smith
Lydia Smith
Owen Smith

Mary Sneed
Julie Southworth
Bob Staib
Frank Stanko
Dorothy Staton

Darlene Stewart
Mark Stipanovich
Herbert Strawbridge
Mark Streza
Eileen Strimpel

Matthew Sugg
Sharmain Sugg
Alice Sullimon
Barbara Sullivan
Jean Sullivan

Mary Conway-Sullivan
Sean Sullivan
Tom and Sandy Sullivan
Robert & Roberta Sunkle
Cher Szeglia

Eleanor Szekely
Nancy Tanis
Barb Taylor
Bill Thompson
Jennifer Thompson

Joanne Thompson
Gerry Tipton
Becky Toney
Angelo Torres
Brenda Torrey

Robert Touber
Bill & Joan Trexler
Judy Uhrina
Fred Unger
V.I.T.A.

Minzat Vagile
Harold Van Niel
Iris Vargas
Jose Vazquez
Lisa Veccic

John Veldhuizen
Carlos M. Velez
Gina Velez
Joanna Velez
Manuel A. Vicario, Jr.

Robin Vigilante
Don Volk
Marian Wagner

Mary Wagner
Mitzi Wagner

Tom Wagner
Joseph Walters
Cindy Ward
Edward Ward
Joseph Ward

Pat Ward
George & MaryLu Wasmer
Lynn Wasmer
Jodi Waterbury
Kathy Watson

Simona Watt

Mary Wehrle
Nicole Weiss
Charles Welsh
Mabel White

Derek Whitmore
Carol Woods
James Yanatsis
Jeff Young
Marilyn Young
Mike Zagata
Kay Zerby
Nathaniel Ziccardi
Robert Ziccardi
Vicki Ziccardi

Bill Zinni
Donna Zinni
Marija Zupancic

We make every effort to keep accurate records. If for some reason your name does not appear, we apologize. It in no way implies that your contribution was not appreciated. We applaud everyone who took part to make our resource development efforts so successful.